THE FIRST LADY
OF MOTORSPORTS
Linda
Vaughn

CarTech®

CarTech®, Inc.
838 Lake Street South
Forest Lake, MN 55025
Phone: 651-277-1200 or 800-551-4754
Fax: 651-277-1203
www.cartechbooks.com

Edit by Wes Eisenschenk
Layout by Connie DeFlorin

ISBN 978-1-61325-232-1
Item No. CT555

Library of Congress Cataloging-in-Publication Data

Names: Vaughn, Linda, author. | Kinnan, Rob, author.
Title: Linda Vaughn : the first lady of motor sports / Linda Vaughn and Rob Kinnan.
Description: Forest Lake, MN : CarTech, [2016] | Includes index.
Identifiers: LCCN 2016009403 | ISBN 9781613252321
Subjects: LCSH: Vaughn, Linda, 1942- | Women automobile racing drivers–United States–Biography. | Automobile racing drivers–United States–Biography.
Classification: LCC GV1032.V28 A3 2016 | DDC 796.72092 [B] –dc23
LC record available at https://lccn.loc.gov/2016009403

Written, edited, and designed in the U.S.A.
Printed in China
10 9 8 7 6 5 4 3 2

Front Cover:
Linda Vaughn is adored by millions of race fans. Here she is on the big gold Hurst shifter.

Front Flap:
Linda Vaughn. (Charles Gilchrist Photo)

Endpapers:
Top left and right are courtesy of Linda Vaughn; bottom left is a Bob McClurg photo.

Frontispiece:
I don't remember this photograph being taken, but I do know that I loved that car and Mother made the outfit.

Title Page:
That's George driving the Chrysler 300H with me on the platform on back, bowing to the crowd. It was freezing cold wherever we were. George loved the Chrysler Corporation and that car.

Contents Page:
Bob McClurg shot this photo of L. V. at the Phoenix AHRA race, while she was reading her new book Here's Linda Vaughn. *Those books now sell on eBay for upwards of $100. (Bob McClurg Photo)*

Back Cover Photos
Top:
James Garner and I, when he won the Baja 1000. Look at him: This must have been after the race and before he had a chance to clean up. Still dirty, but oh my, what a handsome man. Every girl had the "warms" for him.

Bottom:
Here I am in the Victory Circle at the USAC Hut Hundred.

Author note: Some of the vintage photos in this book are of lower quality. They have been included because of their importance to telling the story.

OVERSEAS DISTRIBUTION BY:
Europe
PGUK
63 Hatton Garden
London EC1N 8LE, England
Phone: 020 7061 1980 • Fax: 020 7242 3725
www.pguk.co.uk

Australia
Renniks Publications Ltd.
3/37-39 Green Street
Banksmeadow, NSW 2109, Australia
Phone: 2 9695 7055 • Fax: 2 9695 7355
www.renniks.com

Table of Contents

DEDICATION 6
ACKNOWLEDGMENTS 6
FOREWORD BY DON GARLITS...............................9

CHAPTER ONE: The Early Days........................... 10

CHAPTER TWO: From Beauty Queen to Spokesperson 26

CHAPTER THREE: The Hurstettes 70

CHAPTER FOUR: The World of Drag Racing .. 84

CHAPTER FIVE: NASCAR.............................. 116

CHAPTER SIX: The Indy 500 138

CHAPTER SEVEN: Formula 1, Sports Cars and More Racing 174

CHAPTER EIGHT: TV, Movies and Celebrities 180

CHAPTER NINE: Awards and Halls of Fame 190

CHAPTER TEN: My Personal Life 204

INDEX 220

DEDICATION

To my mother, Mae Vaugh, Betty "Booper" Drye, and
Greg Chamberlain. The three loves of my life!

ACKNOWLEDGMENTS

from Linda

Let me start from the beginning; I want to thank God Almighty and Jesus Christ because I am a Christian and I believe in angels, and my dear mother Mae Vaughn, who was my first angel. I made my mother a promise that since she took care of me while I grew up, I would take care of her and that she would never be cold or hungry again. I bought her a house, cars, and took good care of her because she took good care of me. I kept my promise when I said, "Mother, I'm going to make you proud of me" and I feel that I have succeeded in making my entire family proud of me. I've worked hard and been dedicated to an industry and a sport that I love so much. I guess you could say that I was married to this industry and sport.

I want to thank my big brother C. B. Vaughn. He really believed in me and bought me my first evening gown so I could be in that beauty contest, and let me come back to Georgia to finish school, and then go on to dental school. And his children: Gerald, Lynn, Brenda, and Sean. I feel like his kids are my kids. I've loved watching them grow up and they've always been there for me, especially Lynny Bin, who was named after me.

And, of course, my big sister Betty Louise Vaughn Miles. I was so proud of her growing up; I used to say, "I'm going to walk and stand like her" because she had the most beautiful figure and I admired her and looked up to her. I'd go shopping and go to the movies with her and I'd listen to how the guys treated her and how she would react. She taught me a lot growing up. She's not only my big sister Betty, she's also like my other mother since my mother passed away. We've become closer and all of Betty's children are like my own children: Gary Wayne, Sherri, Michelle, Amanda, Amy, Ashley, Katie, Carley, and Anna Mae.

Then there are Sherri's children. They're also just like my own children; I love them and I'm so proud of them. I spend every holiday that I possibly can with them, especially Christmas. But we're such a big family that we need to draw names, if you know what I mean. It's hard to buy 57 gifts when you're only one single old maid like my niece called me last Christmas. She said, "Aunt Linda, I want to be like you when I grow up. I want to move to California and be an old maid like you!" But I'm not an old maid. I really am a hard-working woman who loves the sport and industry and I've always wanted to make my family proud of me. I miss seeing them.

And then there are my twin half-sisters Sheila Ann and Shirley Jan, from my mother's other marriage. I want to thank them for believing in me and supporting me and going with me to the races.

It's amazing; everyone in my family became a race fan, except for my daddy, Seabrun Broderick Vaughn. Daddy looked like John Wayne, was married numerous times, and was quite the man about town. He was very handsome, very smart, and a great sheetmetalist. We were never close when I was growing up but it was good to get a daddy, finally, at 40 years old. My father became really interested in who I thought was going to win a race and he'd go down to the local barber shop and bet the boys. And 99 percent of the time he would win, because I was pretty astute and knew who was going to win. It was fun watching him.

All of the Vaughn family; I could go on forever naming them. I have a slew of cousins. I'm one of the Vaughn Clan from Dalton, Georgia, and I'm proud of it.

I want to thank George Hurst and Jack Duffy for being so proud that I represented them in NASCAR, NHRA, Indy-Car, off-road racing, Formula 1, and all of the different forms of racing we were involved in. They were like family to me and we had a wonderful experience all those years.

There has been some sadness and lots of happiness, from the winner's circle to the funerals, but that goes with the territory, unfortunately. I've lost a lot of loved ones and we've also saved a lot of lives with our Jaws of Life that George Hurst invented. George and Jack, my hat's off to ya'll for believing in my gray matter and supporting me and buying me all those costumes that my mother made, and for believing in the fact that we could make Hurst a household name, which we did.

That was exciting. Even today, I go places and people know me as Miss Hurst Golden Shifter. I'm so proud of the original Hurst shifter and know "I promoted that" or "I was there in that victory circle."

It's been a lovely racing family, but I want to also thank Chevrolet, SEMA, PRI, the Mecum and Barrett Jackson auctions, and all of the Halls of Fame and other organizations that I've been so proud to be a part of and represent.

And I also want to thank Tom Siefker for working with me for 35 years at Indianapolis Motor Speedway.

When CarTech, Wes, and Rob brought me the proposal to do this book, I was really excited and still am, and I sure hope you folks enjoy it. I want to thank everyone for all of the support we had for the photography, and from my friends and racers for their beautiful comments.

The tears we shared, the hugs we shared . . . I could go on and on and on, but I'm sure you all want to read more and know more, so I hope this leads me into the next book coming down the road. I'm not through yet folks, I've only just begun!

Thank you all. God bless, and God bless America.

from Rob

After 27 years in automotive publishing and holding the editor's chair at several different magazines over the years, including *Hot Rod*, I often wondered just what it took to write a book about anything involving my passion, which is cool and/or fast cars and the racing world in general. Many of my colleagues had done it with various levels of success, but I never really had a strong enough desire to take one on, until CarTech contacted me about writing this book with and about Linda Vaughn.

I first met Linda Vaughn in the early 1990s at the SEMA Show in Las Vegas. As is customary for the past few decades, after the show wraps up for the day, everyone gravitates to the Las Vegas Hilton Casino bar. It was there that I struck up a conversation with Angelo Giampetroni of Ford Racing. As we were talking about a project idea, up walks Linda Vaughn. As I was retrieving my jaw from the floor, Angelo introduced us, and it was like she had known me for 30 years. Of course I knew who Linda was. My *real* education began in the eighth grade, reading *Hot Rod* and *Car Craft* magazines during study hall (and usually during class too), so I knew all about Miss Hurst Golden Shifter by the time I hit puberty.

Having turned down many offers to pen books based on technical subject matter, when Wes pitched me the idea to do a book not just on, but with, Linda I jumped at the chance. So first off I have to thank my CarTech editor, Wes Eisenschenk, for giving me the chance to work on this book, for his incredible patience with my tardiness with the copy, and for tracking down a lot of the photography and usage rights. Sorry, Wes; but it's a great book!

Of course, thank you to the First Lady of Racing herself, Ms. Linda Vaughn. She took me into her home and made me feel a part of her family, which is the personality trait that I heard about from everyone I spoke to during the course of the book. A beautiful woman doesn't last nearly 60 years in the male-dominated world of motorsports without having that "something special," and Linda most certainly does. When you get to know her, she is far more than just a pretty face. This woman knows her marketing and the products that she's representing better than many so-called "experts," and her breadth of knowledge of the different types of racing is unparalleled. I'm also incredibly envious of her ability to not only remember everyone's name, but also details about them and where she met them. Someday, hopefully in the distant future, scientists really need to study her brain and figure out how she does it, because she doesn't even really understand how.

I would also like to thank all the legendary racers that I got to spend some time with for the book, even if it was sometimes just by phone or email. Roy Hill, Shirley Muldowney, Don Prudhomme, Al Unser Jr., and all the rest have been lifelong heroes to me. For them to let me get inside their head for just a few minutes is something I'll never forget and always be grateful.

My thanks to the contributing photographers and their collections of outstanding Linda Vaughn images and thoughts, including Bob McClurg, Andy Shapiro at Hurst Corporation, Howard Koby, Meeka Cook, Tommy Erwin, Fred Von Sholly, Charles Milken Jr., Wayne Andrews, Bruce Mehlenbacher, Bob Wenzelburger, Todd Wingerter, Allen Tracy, Charles Gilchrist, Paul Stenquist, Bill Truby, Mike Mikulice, Hugh Baird, Gregg Doll, James Handy, Mike Cox, David Smith, Will Cronkite, John Hilger, Tom McCrea, Courtney Hansen, Doug Peacock, Kevin Hughey, Arie Luyendyk, Robbie Robertson, Bob Boudreau, Don Smyle, Doug Boyce, Steve Reyes, Alan Eaerman, Racing Research Center, Jim Senkewitz, Todd Trapnell, Tami Pittman, Shelley Harmon, Marsha Bennett, and most of all Tom Siefker, whose meeting at PRI I was forced to miss due to day-job duties. Tom has been Linda's personal photographer based in Indianapolis for many years, and his contribution was most helpful.

Finally, all my friends and colleagues that knew I was working on the book and encouraged me throughout the process and helped push me to meet the deadlines that I constantly missed (sorry again, Wes!). Any project of this magnitude requires a strong support group, and I'm thankful I had that.

Linda Vaughn

VW SHIFTER

HURST SAF-T-TRIGGER

TRIGGER DOWN   TRIGGER UP

1   3   1   OUT

2   4   R   2

WARD SPEEDS   REVERSE & ROCKING

BEST NEW PRODUCT

MISS HURST GOLDEN SHIFTER

JEEP 4   HURST   ARMED FORCES CLUB

The variety of work with Hurst was always something I looked forward to. Whether it was seminars, working with the Armed Forces Club or downtime with George and June, there was always a smile on my face.

FOREWORD
by Don Garlits

Linda Vaughn has been my friend for many years. She came from a little country town in North Georgia by the name of Dalton, and it just so happens that my very first introduction into speed parts was from one of her classmates, Grady Pickle, also from Dalton. Grady drove a hopped up 1938 Ford convertible, with an Edmunds dual-carburetor manifold, purchased from none other than "Honest Charlie" in Chattanooga, Tennessee. Grady and I worked together at Ferman Chevrolet during my early automotive years.

Grady and I visited Dalton one winter to see his parents over Christmas. I first met Linda during this visit, and she was a sweet, young country girl, just as she is today. I am always impressed when fame and fortune don't change a person. I remember well the advice given to me by the old lady who lived next door to us during the 1930s. She always said, "Treat the people nice on

the way up the ladder, as you will face them all on the way down!" I can't count the number of times Linda has stood in the Victory Circle with my crew and me at the NHRA national events. Even at the end of a very hard day (and week, for that matter), Linda was always smiling. In fact, I have never seen her frown.

She was engaged to a general for a short period of time and sported a 15-carat diamond, the biggest one I have ever seen! She was also married to a famous racer, but that also went away after a while. I guess that not many men could stand the fact that Linda was well endowed and all the other men took a real good look! Personally speaking, I would not have minded at all, as long as I knew she was all mine. Let 'em look, just don't touch. "She is all mine," would have been my answer.

A lot of people don't know that Linda Vaughn was the NASCAR Queen for a few years, before coming over to drag racing. Boy, I am glad she did and so are millions of drag racing fans! I can't even imagine drag racing without Linda. She is drag racing, and always will be. Even today, retired for many years, she draws a large crowd anytime she makes an appearance and the autograph line will stretch out for quite a distance. It is rumored that during her NASCAR tenure, she was water skiing in the Atlantic when the top of her two-piece bathing suit came off and was gone forever. The boat driver had a hell of a time getting Linda back to shore without causing a ruckus!

She worked for Hurst Shifters for many years and George Hurst saw the value that Linda added to his product line. Looking back, it seems that Linda was always Miss Hurst Shifter. Kind of like I am "Dodge-powered" forever. It says a lot about character, when a company keeps a celebrity over a very long period of time, and the celebrity stays with the sponsor for many, many years. Linda is just such a person and I am proud to call her my friend for life.

1 THE EARLY DAYS

My grandmother used to start all my bedtime stories with "Once upon a time." So . . .

**Was I glamorous, or what? This was my Mae West pose.
"Why don't you come up and see me sometime?"**

Once upon a time, there was a little blonde-headed girl named Linda Faye Vaughn from Dalton, Georgia. What began with a humble, average childhood has led me down a path that I never would have dreamed I would walk. One that I wouldn't trade for any path to any destination in the world. But I need to start at the very beginning.

Growing Up Vaughn

I was born in 1942 to Seabrun and Mae Vaughn, the youngest of three kids. My daddy was a big ol' handsome man; he looked like John Wayne. He was born in 1913 and my mother in 1918; they got married in 1932 when my mother was 14. Back then in the South, people got married real young. They had a boy first, C. B. Vaughn Jr.; Daddy's name started with an S (he was Big Seab) so they changed it to a C, and Broderick was the doctor that delivered all of us kids. We didn't call my big brother Cebrun, though; he's C. B. Then they had a daughter, Betty Louise, and then I came along later.

Daddy never went to a race but he watched them on TV, and he liked Dale Earnhardt. Daddy was part of the Vaughn clan, all good lookin' guys and hell-raisers, and they pretty well ran the town. Grandpa was the sheriff and everybody was afraid of him, and Daddy was a sheetmetalist at Dalton Sheetmetal Company. Dalton was known as the Carpet Capital of the World and it was a booming town in the 1940s.

Daddy also raised fighting roosters and, just as you'd expect in the 1940s South, the Vaughns also made liquor. All the folks making moonshine had their own specialty, and Daddy was known for his peach brandy.

Being the good-looking, hard-living rascal that he was, Daddy hopped around a lot, if you know what I mean. He was a man about town, and I think I was my mother's love child trying to save that marriage. But then the war started and some of the boys went off to war while Daddy stayed home working as a sheetmetalist.

One day, a company in Detroit called him to come up and work for them and he left us there in Georgia. My mother had to go to work as a seamstress

This is maybe the first photo ever taken of me. This is with my mother right after I was born, and Daddy was already living up in Detroit. Mother was so beautiful, and look at those slacks. The car behind us was Mother's 1940 Ford that she drove to work and back, and I'd sure like to have that car. I gave her a model of a little 1940 Ford years ago and she gave it back to me before she died. I still have it, but I never did get to buy a 1940 Ford for real.

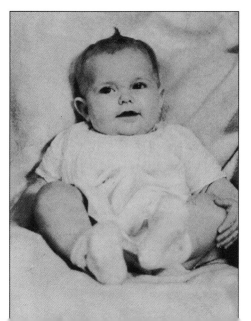

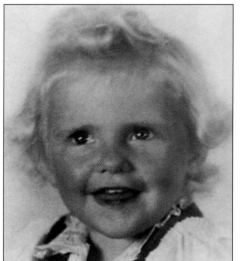

I guess I was about a year old here, and now that I see this photo I look just like my nieces Brenda and Lynn did at that age. I was a cute little thing, wasn't I? My curly blonde hair started really showing.

At six months old and with that little cowlick of hair, I look like a young Alfalfa from "The Little Rascals."

Here I am at around 3½ years old, and I look a little cocky don't I? There's a little attitude there, but the photographer must have said something to me to get that look on my face.

at a hosiery company making parachute strings out of nylon. She'd take me to work with her and I'd sleep in a little box while she sewed.

Eventually Daddy came back, but they ended up getting divorced. Like I said, Daddy was a good-lookin' man and he liked to hop around, and he got a girl pregnant up in Detroit and married her. I have a half-sister named Cheryl that I've only seen two times in 40 years. She's a beautiful blonde; 6-feet-tall and gorgeous. The last time I saw her was in the early 1980s when she came to the Detroit Auto Show to see me when I was working for Gratiot Auto Supply. You see, Daddy disowned her because she married a black doctor, which was *not* allowed in the South! Oh no! So I've lost touch with her and I've tried to find her through social media but I haven't been successful. Cheryl Dunbar was her name after she got married. I'd love to find her.

Always a little ornery, I climbed under the porch and cut my hair off, so Mother took me to the beauty shop to get my hair styled.

Here I am at five years old.

When Mother and I moved to the next house and lived alone around the time I was in first grade, the house and neighborhood were both worse, and they were very hard times. This is when I had to walk through the rough part of town to get from school to our little house. But Mother provided for me, that's for sure.

We grew up next door to my aunts Ruby and Peggy and their kids and grew up as a tribe of Vaughns. We were always together, especially when there was a birthday party for one of us. This is my party, I think, when I was 7, with me in the middle of all the cousins.

Here am I at 8, starting to grow into the little fireball that I eventually became.

We eventually moved out of that house and into the projects, in a little bigger house with a small yard. This little dog was named Corky. It hung around for a while and we fed it, and I got to play with it a lot.

That's my grandmother Maude, my uncle Sam, one of my cousins, and I at my birthday party. Grandmother Maude was a Vaughn from my daddy's side of the family.

This is me at about 8 years old. I think the reason I wasn't smiling is because my front tooth had fallen out.

This is me at 12 years old, after my sister took me to the beauty shop for a permanent.

Mae Vaughn

My mother raised me while working two jobs, and we lived next door to her sisters, my aunt Ruby Townsend and aunt Peggy Hunsucker, who had five kids. Because we all lived next door to each other, I grew up with a bunch of little cousins and was a real tomboy. I watched a cat climb a tree once and thought, "I can do that," so I climbed trees. I was like that cat and could get up a tree faster than anybody.

There was playtime for sure, but I was always working. I grew up helping my mother and aunts in any way I could; it's just what you did back then. As I walked to school I would collect Coca-Cola bottles, save them up and wash them, then take them down to the store on Saturday and make a nickel or a dime and go to the movie on it. I was marketing even back then! I'd do odd jobs and save my money for things I wanted.

That's my mother and I at the International Motorsports Hall of Fame banquet. George Bush was there. When I came downstairs in that outfit, Mother told me I looked more like an angel that night than she'd ever seen me. I presented the Racing Angel Award and she loved it; she was so proud.

There's a very serious conversation going on right here. "Mother, come meet me at the barn, we're going to have a discussion." You know how you sometimes say "meet me behind the barn" and it means, "I'm going to whip your butt"? With Mother and I we met at the barn to have deep conversations. This was in 1986 when I told her I was getting a divorce, and I wanted her to know in my heart where I was coming from.

This is my sweet mother and I at the car show with the Hurst Olds Club of America. A lot of people called Mother Mrs. Mae, and I was so proud of her that night. We had a great time.

What a wonderful photo of my whole family: me, Mother, brother C. B., sister Betty, sisters Sheila Ann and Shirley Jan, and my sister-in-law Barbara Nell in the back. The little girls live in Mississippi, and this was on Easter.

Look at that handsome brother of mine! He had more women at his funeral than anyone else, even the famous race car drivers I knew! And my sisters Shirley Jan and Sheila Ann; Sheila Ann loved drag racing and Shirley loved Richard Petty and John Force; she fell madly in love with Force. He sent her a John Force Racing leather jacket; I don't even have a John Force Racing leather jacket!

When Richard Petty won the race in Atlanta, Shirley was standing in Victory Circle with me and he gave his goggles to her (back then, they still wore open-face helmets and goggles). She still has them.

Both sisters live in Ripley, Mississippi, and have children.

This is at my house in California, where I still live, one of the times Mother came to visit. She was so proud of me getting all of those awards, but I told her "I'm just a chip off the old block, Mother!" The cat is my only child, Snow.

Mother and I with Bobby Yowell's Plymouth Duster.

For instance, our neighbor was a traveling salesman and he didn't have a washer and drier, so he'd give me a quarter a pair to wash his socks. I'd wash 'em, but since I was too small to reach the clothesline I'd pair them up and hang them on the fence to dry. I'd hide my money and then I'd go buy myself something nice, or go to the movies. I've been that way all this time, always working and hiding my money.

I gave Mother a fox fur stole for Christmas and I was in my black and white checkered jacket. We looked hot in our new furs!

I hadn't developed until 14 and it drove me crazy because I wanted a figure like my big sister. But it eventually came and boy, howdy! This photo was taken when I was 14. I struck this pose and thought I looked so cute standing there. I tell you, I thought I was hot stuff!

Sweet 16 and never been kissed!

When I started junior high school, my mother met a man who eventually became my stepfather, Kenneth Lee Jeffcoat, and we moved to South Carolina, which was where he was from, and they had twin girls, my sisters Sheila Ann and Shirley Jan Jeffcoat. I was 12 when they were born and I admit I was a little jealous of them. All of a sudden, I wasn't the little baby anymore; they were the babies. And I did *not* like South Carolina, I didn't like where he was from, and I didn't care for that type of lifestyle. I was miserable there and told my brother C. B. that, so he came and got me and I went to live with him and my grandmother for a while back in Georgia, and that's where I went to high school.

These photos are from my first professional photo shoot, right before high school graduation. I went to Owens Mills Photo, and paid for them with my money from working in the dental office. By this time, I had already met Jimmy Newberry and fell in love with his 1957 Chevrolet and drag racing! I was tempted to drop out of high school, but I was determined even then to always finish what I started and I graduated with honors. Don't I look so formal in the cap and gown?

C. B. Vaughn

My brother was my everything. He was like my big brother, my father, and mentor all rolled into one. He worked for my daddy in the sheet-metal business and always stood up for me. You see, Daddy was never really that nice to us kids. He was tough, a real tough old bird. And his daddy, Grandpa Sam A. Vaughn, Old Man Sam was his nickname; well, everybody was scared to death of him. But I wasn't scared of him at all. I liked him because he was meaner than snakeshit and I was a wiry little thing.

"C. B. taught me how to 'take my part,' meaning stand up for myself."

My handsome brother C. B. Vaughn and I. He would go to races and events with me sometimes, and would end up signing autographs for all the girls there. Everybody thought he was Richard Egan, the movie star, but he'd say, "I'm C. B. Vaughn. I'm Linda's brother."

During my junior high school years, my mother and I moved to South Carolina with my new stepfather Kenneth Lee Jeffcoat, where they had two little girls, my half-sisters Sheila Ann and Shirley Jan Jeffcoat. But I didn't like living there at all, and told C. B. that, so he came and got me to come live with him and my grandmother in Georgia. This photo was him and me with his Ford Galaxie on the day he picked me up.

My mother and my brother C. B. at my apartment in Atlanta in February 1969.

C. B. taught me how to "take my part," meaning stand up for myself, if necessary, because I was a girl and walked by myself after school. Or I'd go down along the creek, called Tar Branch, and walk along the rocks to avoid trouble. But he taught me to pick up a rock or something and keep it in my pocket, in case I ran into trouble. "You don't want to break your hand Weenie." C. B. used to call me Weenie, or sometimes Frankfurter, because I loved hot dogs and ate them all the time; foot-long hot dogs with coleslaw.

Betty Louise Vaughn Burch Miles

Betty Louise (I called her Bet-Bet sometimes) is like my best friend, mother, and sister all rolled into one, especially since I lost my mother and brother. When I was a little girl, I'd come to visit her because she went to live with Daddy and I lived with my mother when my divorce happened. We'd see each other some holidays.

She was a tough one to get to understand racing. She didn't quite understand where I was coming from and what I was doing, yet people would stop in at Daddy's El Ranchero and get a hamburger and a beer from my sister Betty (she ran the place for Daddy). It was the best hamburger and beef stew in town, and Betty would say, "Where ya'll going?" and they'd say, "We're going to the races to see your sister."

So she kept kind of asking about it until one time Mother said, "Okay Bet, I'm taking you to Daytona." It took one trip to the Daytona 500 and my sister Betty fell in love with her little sister, who worked hard and made her proud. After that, my pictures were up on the wall in Daddy's little sports bar and she'd say, "Yeah, that's my little sister. Yeah, I went to the Daytona 500. I know David Pearson, Richard Petty, Fireball Roberts, Smokey Yunick." She fell in love with it and we really became friends after that.

She was a little jealous of me in the beginning. She told me once that when I was born she wasn't the baby any more and she got mad at me. I'm

This is my sister Betty Louise, with me outside Grandma Maude's house in Dalton, Georgia, when she took me to get a permanent.

Here's my sister Betty Louise Vaughn Burch Miles (Betty Boop or Bet-Bet) and my little niece Sherry. Betty makes the best cornbread in the South!

That's my sister Betty Louise Vaughn with her hand on her hip and holding my hand, and my cousin on the left. Betty would take me with her sometimes when she went into town or wherever. She always had to babysit me; I was such a little brat!

really proud of Betty; she's my real true big sister. I love her dearly and she's also my mentor, a very wise ol' Southern girl, let me tell you. When she says things you can best believe it's going to be the truth whether you want to hear it or not!

All of my racing friends, including Raymond Beadle, just loved her; Snake thought she was as cool as could be. They all liked Betty because she was the Annie Oakley of the family. When you go up that mountain road to her house, you'd better call and let her know you're coming because if she doesn't know you're coming, she will greet you with a big ol' shotgun. She's a real character. Her children are like my children.

Betty has many memories of growing up in our family. "We didn't have a lot of money growing up. Mother made most of our clothes. Linda started going to beauty pageants and Mother made these beautiful dresses. I remember one time we went to a club called Zoe's. All the racers were there. Fred Lorenzen, Fireball Roberts, David Pearson; and everybody loved Linda. I was talking with David and he asked who was going to win the race and I told him he was.

"I offered him a piece of Juicy Fruit gum and he took it. He went out and won the race. And the next time I saw him he asked me for another piece of gum! We ended up dancing with those guys and Fred was the best dancer.

"Whenever Linda comes back home to Dalton she always tells me we're not going out for fried chicken. The first thing we do when she comes home is we go out for fried chicken!

"We're all so proud of her, though we wish she would move back home."

Shirley Jan and Sheila Ann

"Linda was a dental technician before she was into racing. Later she fell in love with the sport and we went with her to all the stock car races. Our mama originated tailgating! She would cook up a bunch of food and we would take it to the races (infield, of course) in the back of the car.

I remember Richard Petty, Junior Johnson, Tiny Lund, and others always came by to get a plate of food. They all called her "Mom," which she absolutely loved! Linda introduced me to my hero, Richard Petty, when I was just a little girl. He was and is such a good role model.

"Linda was a great role model. She not only loves the drivers but their families as well."
— *Shirley Jeffcoat Thompson*

"My first memories with Linda were of all of us going to the stock car races. Like Shirley said, Mother was always fixing something up to eat at the races for everybody. Tiny Lund, Fireball Roberts, Fred Lorenzen and others would all stop by after the races and grab some food. Kyle Petty and Davey Allison were there too, and younger, like us. Davey called Linda 'Aunt Linda' and she loved it.

"Over the years Linda took us to the drag racing events where we got to meet Bill 'Grumpy' Jenkins, Larry Lombardo, Ed McCulloch, Don Garlits, Ronnie Sox, and all the drag racers.

"I don't see Linda ever slowing down. We'd all like her to, but she doesn't know how!"
— *Sheila Jeffcoat Franklin*

"Betty Louise (I called her Bet-Bet sometimes) is like my best friend, mother, and sister all rolled into one."

This is my wonderful grandmother and grandfather. That's Benjamin Franklin Mullinax; my mother was a Mullinax before she married a Vaughn. Grandma and grandpa were both Irish, ticklish, and meaner than snake doodoo! Grandmother died pretty early so I didn't really know her, but Mother told me stories. My daddy was Old Man Seab and they called grandpa Old Man Ben, and he was meaner than hell, but I thought he was sweet. He had one brown eye and one blue eye and used to take me fishing and on picnics; him and I were pals. He used to tell me, "You're going to be my movie star."

Growing Up in the South

Georgia was segregated back then and it could be a pretty scary place. But I've never been racist. I always thought "to each his own." I don't care if it's nice black folks or nice white folks, but there's nothing worse than a bunch of rednecks or bad people. It never has been about skin color to me, it's all about the content of your character, like Martin Luther King said.

I always treated people fairly and nice and we had a lot of black folks in Dalton. I'd even sneak off and go to the black church. Rooster was the preacher and he was a good friend of my daddy's. He was great and I liked him; I enjoyed his music and his preaching. We grew up going to church; I mean what else were you going to do on a Sunday in Dalton, Georgia? I loved the sweet Southern Baptist churches but I never did like those holy rollers with the snakes and all that stuff. That was scary and too over the top for me.

I could take care of myself in scary situations, and I could shoot a gun at a young age. Grandpa told me once that if I ever saw a mad dog to pick up a piece of stovewood or something to protect myself. Have you ever seen a mad dog? They walk sideways and are foaming at the mouth and are just crazy.

One time I was out in the yard with my twin sisters when they were just little girls, and they were playing under the Concord grapevine when a mad dog came in the yard and started going for them. It was going to bite my sisters and it scared the hell out of me, so I ran in the house and asked Grandpa where the shotgun was. He asked, "Can you even hold it? Do you think you can really shoot him?"

I could hardly pick it up but I told him, "I know I can; damn sure I will." I blew that damn dog's head off, killed that sumbitch.

Like I said, C. B. acted as my father while I was growing up. I really got to know my father when I was 40 years old and going through my divorce and the hard times that went along with it, and I really missed having him in my life.

As a young girl, I always missed having a daddy for things like PTA meetings, football games, fathers' day at school, going on picnics, going to church . . . you know, just having a daddy. I missed it. But when I was having some problems in later life, he stepped up and took care of some stuff in the good old-fashioned Southern way, if you know what I mean, and we became closer then. But it took a long time, that's for sure. That was also the first time he ever told me he loved me.

Meeting Big Daddy

"Big Daddy" Don Garlits was the first drag racer I ever met. His best friend was Grady Pickle, who lived in Dalton, and Garlits would come up to Grady's house and work on the engines. One day when I was 14, I rode my bicycle over to Grady's house to see what was going on and he introduced me to Big Daddy. When they got done working on the engines, they'd go out on the

That's my daddy, Pop Pa Seab, the first time he came out to California. We went to Las Vegas and had a big suite at the Sands hotel comp'd for all of us, and he had a big round bed all to himself and he loved it. I was 40, and this was the first time in my life that he told me he loved me. He died in 2004 and I miss him terribly.

street and run them. But my grandmother ruled the roost and would only let them run when the trains were running through town.

You see, she was selling moonshine at the time and didn't want any attention drawn to her operation, so she'd only let those loud Top Fuel dragsters run when the noise would be drowned out by the noise from the trains. I think watching Grady and Big Daddy work on those cars is what started my addiction for racing. I saw him the next year and I was bustin' out all over and he just couldn't believe how I'd grown up!

Bobby's Drive-In

When I got into high school, I started to develop as a young woman but I didn't have a boyfriend. I had a lot of guys chasing me and wanting to carry my books down the hallway, but I'd carry them tight in front of me so that they couldn't get to me. I didn't really like any of the boys I went to school with and just wasn't interested in dating any of them, but one day I went to a drag race and saw a 1956 Chevrolet and loved it. It belonged to an older boy named Jimmy Newberry. We talked and flirted a little bit, and I could tell he liked me and I kind of liked him.

I'll never forget going to a football game at Dalton High and who was sitting behind me but Jimmy Newberry and Jackie Mitchell. They both had 1956 Chevrolets and I loved those cars. Anyway, I was sitting in front of them and every time I'd jump up and holler they'd check me out. I had the big boobs but I also had a cute little tushy, so they couldn't help but look! So we talked and flirted some more, and I saw him at the dragstrip a little bit after that. He was real sweet and invited me out for a double date with my cousin Poochie and Jackie, and Jimmy and me. We went to a movie and then went to Bobby's Drive-In afterward.

Whenever you went to Bobby's Drive-In, after you've had your milkshake and hamburger, there's going to be a drag race! They were building Interstate 75 back then and you could go up on it before it was finished. It was exactly a quarter of a mile from one bridge to the other bridge, so we'd race bridge to bridge every Saturday night as we left Bobby's Drive-In.

Forrest Schropshier came up with his *Milk Wagon* car. Robert Nance from Calhoun, Georgia, came up with his Chevrolet. Charles McFarland had this ugly red 1957 Chevrolet with a Continental kit and big old heavy fender skirts on it. Jimmy had gone and bought himself a black two-door 1957 Chevrolet fuel-injected car and, well, I was madly in love. My first true love of a car was that 1957 Chevrolet Bel Air with fuel injection.

I couldn't drive yet, so Jimmy taught me and right off the bat I was a natural at pushing in the clutch and shifting gears. The gear shifter in the car was all wobbly and hard to use. So I went to Honest Charlie's Speed Shop just up the road in Chattanooga, Tennessee, and bought a Hurst Competition Plus 4-speed shifter for Jimmy's car. Honest Charlie himself let me open a charge account and I paid $5 down and $5 a week for it. That was my very first entry, so to speak, into the automotive aftermarket world where I've spent the rest of my life.

The Hurst shifter was a lot tighter and smoother than the stock one, and we'd go drag racing from bridge to bridge every Saturday night. We got busted one night and they took us to jail, and boy, oh boy, did I get in trouble. Daddy came down and checked on me because he knew all the police officers. He was back in Georgia by then and he was pretty mean to me; I

"I think watching Grady and Big Daddy work on those [Top Fuel dragsters] is what started my addiction for racing."

This was my first full-length blonde mink coat that I bought myself so I'd never have to give it back. It was my gift to myself, and I had it made at Ben Douglass Furs in Charlotte, North Carolina.

"The Vaughns were hooked on racing, and I think they all really loved that whole era. I know I did, and still do. I'm never going to grow up!"

> 66 I had seen Linda once before, from a distance, before I actually met her. She was probably the best-looking thing in North Georgia at the time. A friend of mine was dating her cousin and he set me up with Linda, and we all rode around together a lot. They had an airport out here that somebody paved and they weren't using it at all. The city let us use it to run cars in about 1958 or 1959. I had a black Bel Air 270 Chevrolet that ran about eight weeks in a row and it was never beaten.
>
> "I respect what Linda has become. I think things worked out for the best that she got out of Dalton because she never could have done that well hanging around this place. She used to ask me, 'What would we have ever done?'
>
> "And I'd say, 'Well, you'd have probably ended up with three or four kids.'
>
> "So yes, it was good for her career and, I think, her life that she got out of Dalton when she did. 99
>
> — Jimmy Lee Newberry

thought he was going to whip me in front of everybody; I was 17. But on the way home he asked me who won the drag race.

On My Own

When I turned 18, I moved out and got a little efficiency apartment in my aunt's old boarding house. I had the top floor and it had a little fireplace and a little couch that pulled out into a bed, and a tiny kitchen and a tiny bathroom. The bathroom was so small and narrow you could hardly wash your hair, but I loved it.

By then I had a job working for Doctor Julian Gregory and Doctor Amos Gregory as a dental technician while I went to school at night to become a dental hygienist, and I really enjoyed that. I thought at the time that my career would be in dentistry, but I was also really enjoying going to the races at Paradise Drag Strip in Calhoun, Georgia, with Jimmy and Huggie Hudgins, who had a Top Fuel dragster.

"Big Daddy" Don Garlits came up a few times and they'd have match races. Huggie was a good little driver. And, of course, we'd run our 1957 Chevrolet and I convinced Jimmy to let me drive because I was lighter and quicker than him. The first time out, I even won my class.

One of the Boys

Jimmy and a half dozen or so of his friends all had 1955–1957 Chevrolets and they formed the Road Ravens club. They'd all drag race down at the dragstrip in Calhoun, Georgia, and all of them became very good drivers. It snowballed for me then; I really fell in love with racing during that time. I'd even go down to the dirt-track races when I was younger and come home with red Georgia clay in my hair and get a whippin'. My mother would say, "What's making you want to go down there? You'll get a whippin' every time!"

But I finally got her to go down there and she liked it too, so I didn't get any more whippin's after that. The Vaughns were hooked on racing, and I think they all really loved that whole era. I know I did, and still do. I'm never going to grow up!

When Jimmy and the boys were done working on their cars, they'd want some beer and stuff so I'd go over to Ridley's and pick up some beer for them, even though I was only 17. You see, I was developed by then and looked older, and I was a Vaughn, so they'd sell it to me. I traded that beer to the guys for the chance to drive the car. "If you can't whip 'em, join 'em," I always said. I became one of the boys even then. They respected me and treated me very nicely. I'd bring them beer but I didn't drink. I wasn't into it. I was into the cars, racing, and learning more.

Eventually, a few of the guys' girlfriends were getting jealous of their boyfriends going to work on cars instead of taking them out, but I told them, "Ya'll got your heads where the sun don't shine! I'm going to cook some chicken, and why don't you make some deviled eggs, and when they take a break from working on the cars and sit down, they'll want to eat and we can become a part of it. They are going to work on their cars whether we like it or not, and they're going to drink their beer and have fun, so why not be a part of it?"

They had the Road Ravens and us girls became the Ravenettes. It was a really sweet group. We all respected each other and had fun, and being a part of it together sure ended all of the jealousy. I knew I wasn't going to have a date with Jimmy on the "boy nights," which was usually a Thursday night, but we'd have a date on Friday and Saturday nights, and maybe Sunday afternoon we'd go to the movie. The key to it was that I didn't compete with them; I joined in and became a part of it.

I was one of the boys. It was so fun growing up back then. I used to say, "I grew up in the 1960s and now I am one." But now I'm in my 70s!

Forever Friends

Jimmy and I dated for 15 years straight. He was my first love, the first guy I had ever kissed or done anything with, and we grew up in a beautiful way. I respect him and I will always love him. I mean that's what love is all about isn't it? When you love someone you never quit. But when I won Miss Atlanta Raceway, he got a little bit upset with me, but he knew I'd always come back home to him.

When I won the Miss Hurst Golden Shifter contest, I told him I was going to move to Charlotte, and when I did that he joined the air force and took off, while I went racing. I would still come home and be with him on the holidays, and he eventually proposed. He gave me a beautiful engagement ring but I chose my career, and he was drinking a lot when he got out of the air force, and I didn't like that.

I grew up in a drinking family. It was a way of life and the Vaughns all bootlegged and had some problems with drinking. It just made me not want to drink, and I think that was the biggest culprit in our breaking up. But we have remained great friends to this day. Jimmy and I will always be great friends. He even got married to a girl named Linda. (I used to tell him, "When you talk about me in your sleep you won't get in trouble because your wife is named Linda too.")

He had a heart issue years later and I went home to Georgia to see him in the hospital, and introduced myself to Linda. So it was a loving, lasting friendship and still is today. He's the reason I fell in love with a 1957 Chevrolet, that's for sure. And I will always thank him for having the patience to teach me how to drive. He's from a wonderful family, the Newberrys and the Adams. His sister Josephine even bought me an evening gown to be in the Miss Atlanta Raceway contest.

I continued to stay friends with his family and his sister. It's a true family love affair with one another. That's the old-fashioned way of being brought up. My family respected his family and vice versa. It all started in that 1957 Chevrolet, though, and if I had it to do all over again I'd do the same thing. When I won Miss Hurst Golden Shifter, I started a marketing career that I still have, and I continue to love the world of automobiles. I didn't want to get married. I was too young. Why would I want to get married? I wanted to see the world, so I took the Hurst job and away I went.

This is Jimmy Lee Thomas Newberry in March 1966, at his sister Josephine's house when I went home for Christmas. I loved that baby grand piano in the background!

Here's Jimmy at his apartment sometime in the 1980s. He's all white-headed now but he's still my first love, and we will always be close.

2 FROM BEAUTY QUEEN TO SPOKESPERSON

Georgia is all about chicken farmers and they had the Miss Poultry Princess pageant, which was the first time I got into a beauty contest. I won it and my prize was a year's worth of chicken. Lord have mercy, I had so much chicken I wouldn't eat it after that!

I was also Miss Dairy Queen once, and then the Miss Atlanta Raceway pageant came about and I decided to try that one too. That's when Jimmy first really doubted my ability. He said, "Oh, you ain't going to win that, you don't have a chance. You're just a little redneck from Dalton, Georgia."

Those were fightin' words and this time I told him, "I'm gonna show you. I'm gonna enter it and win." It also made his sister Josephine mad so she bought me the prettiest evening gown for the pageant. I won Miss Atlanta Raceway and told Jimmy to stick it where the sun didn't shine. And I was kind of on my way.

Miss Atlanta Raceway

I had grown up watching the race promoters build this really big, beautiful track because it wasn't that far away, and when I heard that they were looking for a race queen I really wanted the job. You see, all of the visiting racetracks were going to have one of their models come in and be in the pageant, so I knew it was going to be stiff competition, but I had friends on the board of directors, Jack and Glenda Black, and they told me I needed to be in the contest. So, I entered it.

That was 1961. They had a bathing suit and an evening dress competition. My mother found a dress on consignment and altered it into the most beautiful Southern Annabella's dress; oh Lord, it was gorgeous! I won Miss Atlanta Raceway. The evening dress was beautiful, but I looked pretty damn good in that white bathing suit too.

"Fred Lorenzen won that first race and when he kissed me in Victory Circle I about fell off of the car!"

The coordinator of the pageant was Marcia Wall, and she also owned a modeling school. Seeing how new to modeling I was, she knew she could help me out and offered to let me come to her modeling school and learn all of the proper ways to walk, sit, talk, and all of that fancy stuff. So I'd walk around with a book on my head and I'd sit like I was having tea. I learned a lot, and she told me, "Linda, I have really high hopes for you. You're going to win but you're going to have to be *very* focused."

And I was; I walked well and I answered my questions well, but when I came out in the bathing suit I think that really got their attention. We closed the show in the evening gowns, and at my first race as Miss Atlanta Raceway

This was my first time at Atlanta Raceway after I won Miss Atlanta Raceway. They wanted me to come out with the evening gown I wore in the contest, and Chris Economaki (with the microphone) introduced me to the crowd. That's the track owner Nelson Weaver next to Chris, the Soap Box Derby winner beside me, and the previous Miss Atlanta Raceway on the other side of me.

This was an ad we did for Atlanta Raceway, sitting on the pace car in Turn 1.

I showed up in that evening dress, then for the parade around the track I slipped into the white bathing suit. That was a hit!

Fred Lorenzen won that first race and when he kissed me in Victory Circle I about fell off of the car! I had never been kissed by anybody but Jimmy and now, Lord have mercy, I got kissed by the great Fred Lorenzen! He was a Yankee and I was a Southerner and it hit all the papers! He won every race and I'd kiss him every time. As you can imagine, Jimmy was jealous as hell but I told him, "Hey, it's in the paper. I'm not hiding anything." I never went out with Fred, I just kissed him in Victory Circle. What's a girl to do? And if I had it to do again, I'd do it again!

Jim Paschal won the first Nashville 500 and I was there (far left) as Miss Atlanta Speedway and also Miss Dixie 400. The girl on Jim's left was Janice Snyder, who was Miss Firebird at the time.

One of my duties (which was in reality more of a privilege) as Miss Atlanta Raceway was to congratulate the race winner in Victory Circle. This was in 1961 at the Dixie 400 when our old family friend Junior Johnson won the Dixie 400 (I was also the Queen of Speed at this race).

Junior is one of my heroes; he was a great driver, but he was also a great bootlegger. My daddy respected him and loved his bootlegging, and he loved my daddy's bootlegging. But they weren't competitors; they were friends. Daddy made peach brandy and Junior made corn liquor, and there's a difference between them. They'd drink each other's liquor because it was the best of the best.

Junior is still my friend and every once in a while he slips me some of the best . . . for medicinal purposes only, of course! Junior's a real great man and if you ever read the Tom Wolfe story "The Last American Hero," you know he has a vocabulary all his own. My roommate was working for John Holman at Holman-Moody and he was driving for them, so we became real good friends and spent a lot of time together at the races. When I needed advice I could go to Junior, but he was more my hero. I really looked up to Junior, I really still do.

This is one of the very first shots of me as Miss Atlanta Raceway. I was such a baby; I hadn't even fully developed yet!

This was at Atlanta Raceway where The Golden Greek, Chris Karamesines, let me sit on his Top Fuel dragster, the first Top Fuel car I'd ever sat on. I was the Queen of Speed and thought I was hot stuff. The Greek used to call me his movie star too, just like my grandpa did. You can tell how happy I was by the grin on my face, but look at the crew; they're probably thinking, "I wish she'd hurry up."

This was in 1964 when I was Miss Atlanta Raceway and this actor (I can't remember his name) kept looking down my shirt. I wasn't real happy about that. I bet he couldn't tell me the color of my eyes!

This was in my Miss Atlanta Raceway days with mechanic Ken Miller.

As Miss Atlanta Raceway, Jack and Glenda Black and I would go to several tracks and participate in the parade lap in our pace car. For the Daytona race, we rode down there in the Pontiac pace car that had *Atlanta Raceway* and *Miss Atlanta Raceway* on the side, with my name, and we'd get in the parade lineup. Before the start of every race they'd have all of the visiting pace cars lined up in order based on the date when their race was.

Our race was next after Daytona, so we were in the front and it was quite a parade. I really enjoyed it. I reigned for a year as Miss Atlanta Raceway, and then entered the Miss Pontiac contest in 1962 and won that, so the next year at Daytona I was Miss Pontiac and Fireball Roberts won. But then I saw the Miss Pure Oil Firebird float and met Booper; that was my next goal.

Look at that young thing at the Atlanta 500, in 1961. I look just like my mother.

Here, left to right, is me, Crash Grant, Bobby McClurg, one of the Goodyear boys, and my friend Judi Judge. Crash always teased me and called me "Emersom," as in "Emersom big boobs you got there, gal."

This is what it's all about folks: in Victory Circle at the Southern 500 in Darlington, 1964, with the great Fred Lorenzen.

66 Two things every driver looked forward to seeing at every race: the checkered flag and Linda Vaughn. 99

— Fred Lorenzen

"I was thrilled that they wanted me to be the next Miss Firebird. I had stars in my eyes and I knew that I could make that into something."

This is when I was Miss Firebird at Chattanooga Raceway with Trotter Pontiac, probably in 1962. Chattanooga was just up the road a piece, and we did an Honest Charlie Speed Shop opening right after that. Mother made me that little red sparkly outfit. Look how high my hair is!

My mother made me this little red dress for me to wear when I'd ride the big red bird around the track as Miss Pure Oil Firebird. It was originally a little longer, but knowing what the crowd wanted to see, she said, "Let's make it a little bit shorter so when you get up there and the wind blows, your legs will show." She thought my legs were my greatest assets.

"Booper," Miss Firebird and the Pure Oil Company

I met Booper, aka Betty Jean Drye, in 1962 and we became best friends right away. Everybody called her Betty Boop, but I called my sister Betty Boop, so Betty Jean became "Booper." Booper worked with Dick Dolan (who passed in 2014, God rest his soul) at the Pure Oil Company and they were very instrumental in my getting a job as Miss Firebird. They had seen how I handled myself at the races and they were interested in me. I was thrilled that they wanted me to be the next Miss Firebird. I had stars in my eyes and I knew that I could make that into something.

Mother made me this outfit too because it was so cold down in Daytona. We went and got all this sequined material and she wrapped it around me, made a pattern, and stitched it up inside out.

This is Smitty, the man who put me up on the big red Firebird and hooked me up to it.

Riding the bird down the front straight at the Southern 500 at Darlington. Oh boy, the Southern 500! That is one rebel-raising, hell-raisin' crowd from the South! Honey, you're talkin' about molasses drippin' off your tongue when you go to that racetrack, and on one side would be white lightning, peach brandy, moonshine of all kinds. But those were some of the toughest, roughest, rebel-raising Confederate-lovin' good folks that I have ever come up against and I was thrilled to death to ride around the track at my first Southern 500. I was accompanied by my sweet mother who also lived in South Carolina, and the twins were there as well.

The next time I rode around that track was as Miss Hurst Golden Shifter and the shifter almost got as much attention as the big red bird.

Firebird was the official fuel for NASCAR, so getting to tour with them was great, and it was a stepping-stone for me to become Miss Hurst Golden Shifter. I had learned so much from the Firebird Company. It was such a wonderful memory; there's nothing like the Southern 500. I was there with Clint Eastwood and Clint Walker and thought I'd died and went to Heaven.

This was at the 1963 Dixie 400 at Atlanta Raceway, with me behind Miss Georgia as we walked through the pits.

This was the Fourth of July race in Daytona, with me, Judy Judge, and Dottie Parker. We girls always had the best tan, because we were staying on the beach. I'd go swimming every day and then go back and do my hair and be ready in an hour, and they just couldn't understand how I could get ready so fast with all that hair. Look how dark Judy is; she was a dear, dear friend of Fireball Roberts, and Dottie of course was my roommate and John Holman's secretary. Sadly, they're both gone now.

Dottie and I during my Miss Firebird days. I still have that flag in my bedroom. Dottie ended up becoming the secretary for Ralph Holman of Holman-Moody, and we were roommates in Charlotte, North Carolina. Ralph provided us a Holman-Moody Mustang and I drove it, because Dottie couldn't drive a stick. Boy, I'd sure like to have that Holman-Moody Mustang again.

So Mother made me a pretty costume and I won Miss Firebird. When I won, I had to go back to Dalton and tell Dr. Julian and Dr. Amos Gregory that I'd been offered the job with Pure Oil Company and couldn't work in the dental field any more. It was only $25 a race but they paid for the hotel rooms, and that was more money than I could make in two weeks at their office.

After I got the job I picked Booper's brain and said, "I'd like to make some costumes. Miss Firebird should be in a costume instead of a bathing suit on the big red bird for the Daytona 500," and she pushed it through for me. That was the beginning of the friendship that endured through all the years.

I lived in Charlotte by then because I thought that was the racing place to be, which it was, and Booper lived in nearby Concord. We ran together the whole time I was Miss Firebird, which was a gas. We went all over, to every NASCAR (National Association for Stock Car Racing) race. She would drive the support car up and they would hook this big red bird behind it, and I'd climb up on the bird, get right in the middle of the wings, and wave to everybody as we went around the track. It was a ritual. And my family fell in love with her.

ARCA president John Marcum giving me a kiss on the cheek at Daytona, and that's Booper with me. This is when those hairnet/scarves were popular in the early 1960s.

With my best friend of my entire life Booper, her daughter Meeka, and two good-looking guys. Who is that standing next to me? When you see this book sir, will you let me know who you are? (Photo Courtesy Meeka Cook)

This is at the Phoenix IndyCar race and Booper is talking to A. J. Foyt, while I'm talking to Billy Vukovich III in the background. We terrorized these two guys and they loved it; they loved us and we loved them. A. J., that cantankerous old Texan, was my first superhero, absolutely the best. Billy Vukovich was from a wonderful family in racing that certainly had some tragedy in their history.

His grandfather Bill won the Indianapolis 500 in both 1953 and 1954 but was killed in a crash in 1955. Bill Vukovich Jr. was the 1968 Rookie of the Year at the Indy 500 and was a master in midget cars. Billy III, qualified for the Indianapolis 500 in 1988. I gave him a party in my Sprite Suite, knowing he was well on his way to a fantastic career. He was Rookie of the Year at the 500 that year but sadly was killed in a sprint car race in Bakersfield, California, in 1990. That boy would still be driving today if not for equipment failure. (Photo Courtesy Meeka Cook)

Booper sitting on this little Alfa Romeo that she loved, which is funny because she complained to me when I bought my Ferrari Dino years later, because it messed up her hair! (Photo Courtesy Meeka Cook)

This is my favorite picture of my best friend in the world, Betty Jean Drye (Booper), and I together. We were talking about a race car driver. You can just imagine what she was saying to me, but I'm going to leave it up to you fans to figure out what she was really saying. It was a really good story! (Photo Courtesy Meeka Cook)

Here's the Three Musketeers again, at what looks like Martinsville Speedway. What a cute group we were, and so skinny! We used to climb up on that Firestone truck in the background and watch the race. (Photo Courtesy Meeka Cook)

This is Booper, me, and Dottie Parker (my roommate, who worked for Holman Moody); we're about to go to the Atlanta 500. I'm pointing to Booper's butt because she got so skinny on us! Can you imagine us three going out? (Photo Courtesy Meeka Cook)

Almost Dying in a Balloon Race!

They have a hot air balloon race every year at the Indianapolis Motor Speedway and we got talked into sponsoring it. George Hurst was into sponsoring everything he could, so we had this big balloon with Hurst written all over it and a big shifter knob. They talked me into going up in it to wave to the crowd. I had a gold lamé outfit and a gold Simpson helmet. I was styling and looked like I was having fun, but I was scared to death!

That's George on the left in the jacket and Jack Duffy in the white shirt in the foreground. Jack was concerned because the wind was blowing very hard that day; you can see it in that flag in the background. Here I look pretty calm, but I was gritting my teeth and muttering, "Are you sure about this?"

Look at the worried expression on George's face. But he just said, "Oh hot shot, you'll be all right." I'm thinking this guy flying the balloon (in the white hat and glasses) doesn't know what he's doing, but I'm going to ride with him!?

It was blowing so hard that when they let go and I got up in the air, we knocked over the outhouse with a woman in it, and she sued us. So my ride was very short. We went up, knocked the outhouse down, landed in the infield, I jumped out, and then told them, "Bon voyage boys, see ya. No more for me!"

I was so mad at George that day. I told him he tried to blow me away! Sadly, the balloon pilot ended up getting killed a month later in a balloon at a race in Pennsylvania. He hit some electrical wires and it electrocuted him.

"Let's make it a little bit shorter so when you get up there and the wind blows, your legs will show." She knew her marketing just as good as I did!

So I went to work for the Pure Oil Company out of Palatine, Illinois; it was a Yankee company. I thought, "Oh Lord, how am I going to work with these folks?" Remember, there was still a North versus South mentality, especially in Southern minds, and there still is today, so a girl from Georgia working for a bunch of damn Yankees was a little bit intimidating. But Dick Dolan was wonderful and Booper was my friend so she kept me posted.

Mother joined the party again and made me a little red outfit with small pleats on it. Knowing what people want to see, she said, "Let's make it a little bit shorter so when you get up there and the wind blows, your legs will show." She knew her marketing just as good as I did!

Mother made all my costumes for years and she went with me everywhere, because I was very young and naïve and she made sure nobody messed

This is when Carroll Shelby met the Booper. You know, Shelby asked Booper to marry him a couple of times. They'd see each other about every 20 years or so. The last time he asked her to marry him, he was real, real sick and told her the truth, saying, "Booper, I'm not doing well and I don't think I have long to live, and I think you deserve more out of life."

He once told my boyfriend Greg, "Ah hell, I'd ask Linda to marry me but she'd a probably killed me!"

The little girl is Booper's daughter Meeka; look how cute she is! (Photo Courtesy Meeka Cook)

Booper and I with good ol' Yankee boy Tom Bigelow. He was a real sweetheart and Booper took to him really well. He was a good racer and ran at Indy in the 1970s and 1980s, but his best success was in midgets and sprint cars. He became a TV announcer in retirement. (Photo Courtesy Meeka Cook)

My brother Lloyd Ruby is one slow-talkin' Texan, but you put him in a race car and he'd pass even A. J. He and Booper both talked so slow they'd get in trouble several times before they said no. This was taken at the Speedway when he came riding up on his motorcycle when Booper and I were standing there, and said, "Come here sister, I want a picture with Booper and you."

Lloyd Ruby should have won the Indianapolis 500 in 1969. Mario Andretti was having problems and that gave Lloyd a chance to win, but a pit stop mistake by his crew punched a hole in the fuel tank when the nozzle stuck, and he was out of the race. That was the year that Mario got his only Indy 500 win. (Photo Courtesy Meeka Cook)

with me. There were some jealous women in the beginning and it was tough, but I let them know right away that I wasn't interested in their husbands, I was there to make a name and represent the Pure Oil Company.

Two of the first people who became my friend were Linda Petty (she often stood up for me) and Judy Allison. These ladies loved me and I loved them, and their friendship made it easier for all the other wives and I to become friends. We just lost Linda in 2014, but to this day all the wives are real close with me. I made them my friends; they respect me and I respect them.

I only had real trouble with one woman, who shall remain nameless, and my momma took care of that in a very Southern way, if you know what I mean. Nobody got hit, but you don't mess with my momma. When the hair on her neck raised up, you were fixin' to get flogged. Have you ever seen a fighting rooster and a fighting hen? When the hen's feathers go up somebody's gonna get in a fight; same thing with a rooster. Momma was a truly sweet, charming, Southern lady, but she knew how to handle a situation when it came up, and when she overheard what that woman said to me, she followed her to the restroom and came out smiling. And we'll just leave it at that. Fireball Roberts (who called me "Bird") saw what was going on and how my momma handled it, and he was really impressed.

I was Miss Firebird for three years and it became real popular because we led the parade before every NASCAR race and we were the official fuel, so I was always in Victory Circle, and Fred Lorenzen got to kiss me some more. Richard Petty won once but I didn't kiss him or the other guys like I kissed Fred Lorenzen. I kissed them on the cheek, just a little peck, you know. I was very well respected then. I've only really kissed somebody like Fred Lorenzen once or twice in my life; those are special kisses. Oh sure, a few guys snuck one in on me when I wasn't expecting, but I'm not telling you who they were!

Linda and Booper, the morning before we went to the Atlanta 500. Mother came out to meet us and Lorne Greene (who was making a special appearance) was there and she said, "These are all my children."

With the great Cale Yarborough in Victory Circle at Darlington in the early 1960s. I was Miss Pontiac here. Look at those stylish little gloves. Cale is a hell of a driver and I also consider him one of my brothers. He and his wife . . . last time I saw him was at Daytona about three years ago and he was looking good. (Photos Courtesy Mike Cox)

I also bought this mink stole. I can't remember what track we were at, but that's Elmo Langley on my right.

When I won Miss Georgia Poultry Princess, I won a trip to Las Vegas and a screen test. I was under 21 so I had to take a chaperone so I took my friend Virginia from Dalton with me. As you can tell, we loved the sun and loved to sunbathe. We had two or three tickets to see Elvis and were even staying on the same floor of the hotel as he was, so we got to meet him. Virginia was madly in love with Elvis, but I just wanted to go backstage. Elvis and his road manager were wonderful to us. This picture was actually taken on the beautiful front porch of Josephine Adams Newberry, Jimmy's sister.

This was a newspaper ad for me as Miss Firebird; I guess to get people to come out and see the races. Those were my measurements then, but certainly not now!

"Call for Phil-ip Mor-Rees!" This was Little Johnny Roventini, the product spokesman for Phillip Morris cigarettes who was barely 4 feet tall but enormously famous. Johnny was discovered while working as a bellboy in New York by advertising mogul Milton Biow, who had the Phillip Morris account. Little Johnny had a 40-year career with Phillip Morris and on TV, and he had a big hand in helping I Love Lucy become a success after Phillip Morris stepped up to sponsor the show. He was a lovely little guy. This is in Charlotte at a race.

This was my first boss, the man who hired me as Miss Firebird, Dick Dolan and his wife Betty Dolan with Booper and I at the NASCAR Hall of Fame in Talladega, Alabama. Dick worked for the Pure Oil Company and was the first man who really believed in my future. And of course Booper worked with me and helped me tremendously to get started.

The things we got me involved in! This was at the Southern 500 at Darlington and I was dressed up as Daisy Mae and that was my billy goat, during the Miss Firebird days. I swear the things the promoters did back then! We had a race with ducks, pigs, and billy goats, and those goats are mean! They'll butt you with their heads, but this one liked me, thankfully. (Photo Courtesy Smyle Media)

At the same Southern 500: They had a costume thing at the track and I got dressed up as Daisy Mae and Buddy Baker was Li'l Abner. We won the contest. I'm a barefooted country girl here, I just wasn't pregnant! (Photo Courtesy Smyle Media)

With the actor Clint Walker at the Southern 500. He was a vegetarian, 6-feet 6-inches tall, very handsome, and a sweet man. Clint was best known as "Cheyenne Bodie" in the television show Cheyenne. (Photo Courtesy Smyle Media)

All of the Pure Oil guys were so nice to work with, and sweet to me. This is Jim, one of the guys that took care of me during my time there. I'm probably whispering in his ear, "Fill my tank please."

There's a smart ass in every crowd! This guy didn't actually touch me or I'da whipped the piss out of him!

When I became Miss Pure Oil Firebird, I got free gas for a year. This was one of the guys we worked with at the Pure Oil Company, doing a promotional photo at Daytona.

See, I do have legs! This was in 1964 during my Miss Firebird days, and I'll bet this guy couldn't tell me what color my eyes were.

Eastern airlines did a promotion for the Golden Falcon and I was one of the celebrities they invited to go on the flight. I always wanted to hold onto a blade of a Golden Falcon service.

This was at a cocktail party at the Detroit Auto Show. Check out my perm.

Betty Jean Drye (known as Booper) and I on the beach at Daytona. Booper was my best friend, the best friend that I will ever have.

I think Booper shot this after I teased up all that hair, making sure she got the can of Aqua Net in the background. At my roast a few years ago, Lynn St. James presented me with a can of Aqua Net with all the drivers' autographs on it.

Miss Hurst Golden Shifter

After reigning as Miss Firebird for three years, the company was bought out and merged with Union 76, and the whole project went down the drain. They brought in one girl for a year to be Miss Firebird after I won Miss Hurst Golden Shifter, Edwina Louise (I called her Winkie Louise). We shared the podium at the races, her as Miss Firebird and me as Miss Hurst Golden Shifter, and we really complemented each other. She would lead the parade and I was the last one in the parade; we were like bookends and we developed quite a fan following.

The three roommates: Booper, Linda, and Dottie. We were something else!

Jack Duffy was the best public relations director in the entire world, and he was the best boss that ever lived. When we first met, we just clicked mind-wise and he became my mentor and almost like my father. Jack gave me away when I got married, and I asked him to take me back when I got divorced! Jack was a brilliant PR man and we were successful together, and also very proud of each other.

This was at what you can consider my "coming out party" as Miss Hurst Golden Shifter at the 1966 Winternationals with Parnelli Jones (left) and J. C. Agajanian (in hat).

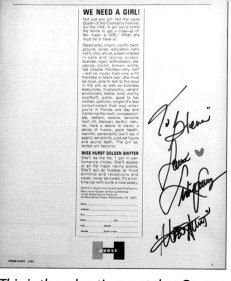

This is the advertisement that George Hurst put in the magazines (this one was from Car and Driver's February 1966 issue) looking for the new Miss Hurst Golden Shifter. Just look at all those requirements, ending with ". . . a jet-set figure and sound teeth." It said that the winner would be "the No. 1 girl in performance circles. She'll appear at all the major racing events. She'll act as hostess at Hurst exhibits and receptions and never, never be bored. It's a full-time job with quite a nice salary." It was right; I was never, ever bored!

These are three of my favorite boys representing Hurst, Airheart, and Schiefer Clutches. From left to right are Howard Maseles, Ron Tilton, and Earl Richey. Howard was The Shifty Doctor for years and years and was so good at it.

This is the day in 1966 that Hubert Platt and I went to Ford Motor Company for these photographs. He signed a deal with Ford and I had our Hurst shifters in the Fords. Put this in your Ford and shift it!

This was taken at another radio or television interview in 1972. We were pretty good at getting the local media to come to the races, and an interview was always a part of it. I was always promoting the races and Hurst! (Charles Gilchrist Photo)

In my standard pose as Miss Hurst Golden Shifter, on the podium and clutching the big gold shifter, bowing and waving to the crowd. This looks like Bristol. The lady riding with me was one of the visiting race queens at the time, and they always rode with me in the parade. (Tommy Erwin Photo)

That's George Hurst driving the Chrysler 300H with me on the platform on back, bowing to the crowd. It was freezing cold, wherever we were. George loved the Chrysler Corporation and that car. Someone just called me to say that they're buying that car to put it in their collection with a bunch of other Hurst cars. The shifter handle is now in the front lobby of the fabulous Museum of Speed in Lincoln, Nebraska. (Fred Von Sholly Photo)

At Hurst we used to make handouts for people, and this was one set up by Jack Duffy. I think this is after we bought Air-heart Brakes and Schiefer Clutches.

Linda

Miss Hurst Golden Shifter

Here you can see Jack Duffy (Monsieur Jacques Dufé, as I like to call him), Ron Tilton, and Earl Richey with Mr. Draper and his wife at the races. Mr. Draper was the CEO of Hurst at the time and approved my Hurst Oldsmobiles, one of which you can see in the background. The Drapers were a lovely couple; they came from Sunbeam Corporation and he also approved my budgets for the year. He was instrumental in Hurst having the official pace car program in 1972, when James Garner drove the car.

Hurst bought Airheart Brakes and renamed it Hurst Airheart. I think this was the first SEMA show we attended with Airheart in the Hurst family. That's Bob Airheart in the glasses, and on the right is Leo Cagan, the president of Hurst and also SEMA.

Leo is 98 years old and still going strong, and goes to SEMA and the luncheon every year. He's still shiftin' gears!

Bob Airheart is 81 now and we still talk every week. Bob was a big part of Hurst Airheart Brakes and he was also a partner with George Hurst. We did a lot of the brakes for Indy-Cars, including those of Dan Gurney, Bobby Unser, and others. Bob eventually started an aftermarket representation business and is now retired, driving his Corvette for fun.

This is my stockbroker Robby Case (right) and Hurst's Al Carpenter (left), after one of them won a dollar bet off the other one. I honestly can't remember who was paying who here, but neither of them liked to lose. Al Carpenter and I did some great promotions for Hurst over the years. Look at my outfit! I found some Hurst material (I can't even remember what it was for) and made pants and a jacket out of it. I was always flying the Hurst colors!

Bob has always called me his sister, and I think of him as a brother. When he was inducted into the SEMA Hall of Fame, he said, "I want to recognize my big sister Linda Vaughn. Thank you for all you have done for me and Hurst Airheart brakes."

I cried that night.

We made a bunch of life-size cutouts of me for promotional displays and they were really popular with fans. I think this photo was at the SEMA show when we gave a customer one of the cutouts. I wonder if he still has it?

George Hurst also supported Soap Box Derby racing because he felt that eventually the kids would grow up to be IndyCar drivers. This was my first Soap Box Derby race and this little Italian boy won it. He was just the cutest thing, and that was a real sweet day.

Linda Vaughn

"Miss Hurst Golden Shifter"

This is another one of Jack Duffy's original handouts. Mother didn't make this costume for me though; it was my first black leather jumpsuit that was made in Hollywood. It's still in my attic somewhere. (Photo Courtesy Hurst Corporation)

Now here is one hell of a group! I'm flanked by A. J. Foyt and King Richard Petty, who were "fighting" over me (wearing one of Mother's gold lamé dresses), while George is just standing there and Ray Truesdale was looking the other way. This was when A. J. was young and gorgeous, Richard is still young and gorgeous, and George who has passed on, but whose spirit still lives with me. These were all such fine gentlemen, and I consider A. J. and Richard both kings.

After I became Miss Hurst Golden Shifter, the new Miss Firebird was Edwina Louise. I called her "Winkie" Louise. Here we are with Paul Goldsmith. I still see him at the International Motorsports Hall of Fame. (Photo Courtesy William Smith)

" Linda was very popular when I was racing. She attended many events with Hurst Shifters. This was from Daytona when I won one of the qualifying races, and as you can see I was pretty happy being in Victory Lane with Winkie and Linda. "

— Paul Goldsmith

Rocky Marciano was a good friend of George Hurst and he came to my party when they crowned me Miss Hurst Golden Shifter. I was so proud and honored to meet Rocky, and he was such a soft-spoken, kind-hearted gentleman, but he'd beat the crap out of you in the ring. I've always liked boxing and good fighters, like Rocky, Thomas Hearns, and Mike Tyson. I like competition of any kind and that's what boxing is, competition.

B&M used to manufacture all of the torque converters with Hurst, and when Hurst got sold again they came out with the Shotgun Converter. This was a promotional and advertising photo for that converter. I put on cutoff jeans and undid a top button on my shirt and we went and shot a converter. I actually shot that gun too. I'm pretty good with a gun.

This is George Hurst and I at the Armed Forces show at the base in Hawaii later that day.

These are the winners from a race somewhere. These guys either worked or won, and if they represented Hurst, George gave them money. Sort of like today's contingency programs in nearly every racing sanctioning body. These were my Hurst Boys.

"Big" Bill France and George Hurst

I was friends with Bill France Sr. from doing all of the NASCAR races, and in 1965, at Daytona, he introduced me to Wally Parks from *Hot Rod* magazine and the National Hot Rod Association (NHRA), and George Hurst. I had actually met them a few years earlier when I was Miss Firebird and they had been watching how I conducted myself at the races, and how I represented the Pure Oil Company. George had his model there, Pat "Perky Patty" Flannery, who was the first Miss Hurst Golden Shifter, but he was looking to change it up a bit.

Mr. France told them that I was out of a job and they told me they were looking for a new Miss Hurst Golden Shifter. George had put a full-page ad in *Hot Rod* magazine advertising the contest, saying you had to have a good personality and you had to like racing. It also said the entrants must have

This was in Hawaii during an Armed Forces show, where we went over to air force and navy bases and put on a show. From left to right is Booper, me, Al Carpenter from Hurst, Lila and George Hurst, and "Mr. GTO" Jim Wangers. Al is telling one of his famous stories. Lila had a wig on that night and asked me, "Is it true that blondes always have more fun?" And look at George. He was always tanned!

" One of my better days with George Hurst . . . Whatever Al Carpenter [third from the left] is saying, I'm not sure I believe it! Meanwhile, a very happy George is enjoying the moment with some of his 'best' friends, including a very pretty Linda Vaughn, who is not sitting next to him! She sure did have lovely long blond hair! "

— Jim Wangers

"solid teeth." I saw the ad and immediately knew I wanted that job, and I certainly had nice teeth because I worked for a dentist, but that comment made me ask George, "Are you looking for a race horse or a race queen?" A little while later, *Hot Rod* magazine publisher Ray Brock called me to say they were indeed going to have the contest. I think they were enamored of what I had done as Miss Firebird. And I could see a future with the Hurst company.

So I entered, along with 199 other girls, and did it all business-like, staying focused like Marcia Wall taught me. And I won. I signed a one-year contract with George Hurst and got a new Pontiac Grand Prix as my company car. I thought I was hot stuff. I pulled into Dalton, Georgia, in that Grand Prix (and later a GTO), all gold and black and just thought I was the coolest thing ever.

It was a very conspicuous car for sure; you couldn't hide in that car. It ran good too. I would drive to the races at Daytona and Charlotte, and my big shifter and its platform would sit on the back of the car when I got there. Then I'd climb up on the platform, grab a little handle on the big gold shifter, and ride around the track waving at people and promoting Hurst Shifters. That was a fun year, and at the end of the year they renewed my contract and I got another car.

With stars in my eyes I moved into a two-bedroom townhouse in Atlanta and Booper moved in with me. She worked for the American Food Purveyor Company, which supplied food to the better restaurants in Atlanta, so we always had great steaks and lobster, a freezer full of food. I loved to cook so she'd bring in the meat and stuff and I'd bring in the vegetables. We were inseparable and lived together for quite a while.

I started traveling to events my first year with George Hurst. I swear he tried to kill me! I had tonsillitis so bad one time, I thought, "I'm not going to make it through this season," but I put up with it until I couldn't anymore and finally had to have my tonsils taken out. The next year we had about 100 events: every one of the NHRA races, NASCAR races, every car show, New York Auto Show, Detroit, Los Angeles. I worked my little butt off and saved my money.

I worked, I worked, and I worked. I lived it. It was my life. My drug was racing. I got hooked on racing and that was my thing. And I could see a

This is another one of Mother's outfits. I got the inspiration from watching Jane Fonda in Barbarella *but I didn't want it "nudey," so first we made a gold bathing suit fit tight, and then went to a fishing store to buy fish net.*

The guys there thought we were crazy and said, "What ya'll goin' fishin' for?"

We said, "Men," as we laughed our way out of the store. (Tommy Erwin Photo)

Joe Schubeck, "Schub," (third from left) was my brother and is still one of my closest friends. The Hairy Olds *sounded like two dragsters when it fired up and would move differently than any other car when it ran, and this car always worried me. It ended up running Joe over and breaking his leg.*

" This is the crew with the Hurst *Hairy Olds* at Riverside. From left to right is Red Hubbard, Hurstette June Cochran, Joe Schubeck, myself, Richard Chrysler, and Jack 'Shifty Doc' Watson. Richard Chrysler used to sweep floors at Hurst and ended up buying the whole company in later years; Red worked for Joe. "

— Linda Vaughn

I remember that this was at Riverside with Joe Schubeck (white shirt and hat) and the Hurst Hairy Olds.

Here's how the fans got to know me, holding onto the big Hurst Golden Shifter and waving to the crowds at racetracks around the country. I never fell off the shifter or had any problems up there, but Jack Duffy and I used to practice having me jump into the backseat just in case something ever happened.

If you look closely you can see a wire running down from the shifter handle to the platform. I would straddle it and sort of use it to brace me as I moved around and waved to people. Well, it popped loosed one time coming out of Turn 4 at the Southern 500, so I jumped into the backseat like Jack and I had practiced while the shifter fell over and I held it. We never actually lost the shifter though, and I never did fall off. (Fred Von Sholly Photos)

future in marketing in the racing and automotive world, with a lot of companies needing help.

George was very tight with General Motors and thought Ford was a four-letter word, but the Fords were kicking butt and I convinced George that we needed to have a shifter in Fords and every other car, not just General Motors. I told him, "If they race and win, you need to have your shifter in the car. Competition is good for you." So we eventually got Hurst shifters in every one of the Big Four cars. We were a great marketing team and really helped make Hurst shifters a household name.

Jack Duffy was Hurst's public relations director and became kind of a father figure to me, while George was like my uncle. Jack knew that I was all alone and still very young, and he knew that I had a lot of decisions I needed to make that could really use some fatherly advice, so he was there for me. And I had brothers from another mother in the Airhearts, after George acquired the Airheart brakes company (which we renamed Hurst Airheart). He also bought Schiefer Clutches and Paul Schiefer became a brother, as did "Gentleman" Joe Schubeck of Lakewood Bellhousings (Joe also drove the *Hairy Olds* exhibition car), and Joe Hrudka of Mr. Gasket. They all became my brothers.

I learned a lot and respected all those guys. The Airhearts and I grew together and did many warehouse shows together. That was a main part of my job as Miss Hurst Golden Shifter; whenever a new parts distribution warehouse or big parts store opened, we would go and represent Hurst and

This was one of our first professional photo studio shoots, with me in the back of the Hurst Hairy Olds exhibition car. Driven by Joe Schubeck, Hairy Olds had two blown Olds engines, one in front and one in back, and it was a push-pull situation. This is as close to being in the car as I wanted to be!

Wearing my Miss Hurst Golden Shifter sash at the race at Pocono. Pocono was one of Jack Duffy and George Hurst's first sponsorships because it was in Hurst's backyard. Jack Duffy got us involved with the Mattiolis who owned and ran Pocono, and it's still family-run. I still go there every summer for a couple of events. Mario has won there. And A. J. and Richard Petty. I went to a lot of races at Pocono.

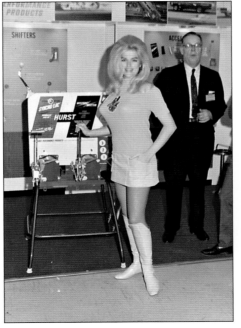

Hurst did several promotions where we would hold a contest and bring the winner and his spouse to a drag race. This was one of them. (Fred Von Sholly Photo)

Representing Hurst Shifters in our booth at the second SEMA show at the Disneyland Hotel in 1968. I had a fit over those boots; I loved them so much! I probably still have them in my attic.

This was at the drags in Bakersfield, California, and I look so tired here. The lady sitting next to me is Susie Kelly, the wife of photography Jim Kelly.

Here I am with Jim Dunn in Bakersfield. Look at those hot rods in the background! California truly was the first home of hot rodding. (Charles Milken Jr. Photo)

Hurst did many auto shows during the year. This was the New York Auto Show and I remember we were just across from the Ferrari display. This dual-engine hot rod sure was different than the Italian cars across the aisle!

educate them and their customers all about Hurst Shifters. And we did a lot of warehouse shows all over the country. When George took over Airheart Brakes, we worked very closely with the brake division in addition to shifters and all of Hurst's other products.

We obviously also worked a lot with racers. Hurst Airheart had introduced a new IndyCar brake setup and we were on our way to the Pocono IndyCar race one year when I asked George if I could invite a couple of racers to visit the Hurst plant on their way to Pocono.

A. J. Foyt was having brake problems in Trenton, so I had him come to the Hurst Performance plant and we blocked off an area for the workers to watch him. You can imagine how cool that was for the workers; the famous A. J. Foyt bringing his IndyCar into the plant and tearing the brakes off it to install our new Hurst Airheart brakes. It all happened right in front of them. It was even better when he won that race at Pocono.

At the end of 1966, George renewed the contract again and said to me, "Alright hot shot, I'm going to make you a corporate employee and you're going to get a ham or turkey every year for Christmas. And I want to give you a pension so that when you retire you're part of our pension." He showed me what I'd get at age 65 if I continued to work for the Hurst Company, but little did I know we'd be sold three times over the years and each time my pension and I went with the sale.

When Mr. Gasket bought Hurst, company owner Joe Hrudka honored the pension, and when he sold the company to Dana, Fred Mancheski also honored it. Then the problems began. Someone stole my pension so I'm without

Win a Date With Linda!

George Hurst was a big supporter of the Armed Forces, and had a contest for military men where we'd bring the winner to the Daytona 500 for a date with me. I was a little bit worried about who might win the contest and asked George, "I don't have to kiss him or anything do I?" and he said not to worry.

The winner was Leonard C. Hobbs who was with the 121st Assault Helicopter Company in Vietnam, and when we found out he was married, we decided to bring his wife too, as a secret surprise. We got them a suite and the three of us went out on a date for dinner, ran around Daytona, and watched the races, and we had a great time. It was like they were on their honeymoon. What a fine couple; they were just lovely.

Contest Winner Leonard Hobbs:

"I may not look like it in this photo, but my head was spinning, my heart was pounding, and my ears were trying to follow the sounds of the cars moving around the track! I knew that me being married meant the Hurst people had to move fast and restructure the 'Date at Daytona' paradigm. That's my wife, Jennifer, on my left, and everyone knows Linda Vaughn. "Winning the contest, leaving Vietnam on a DC-8, stopping in San Diego to pick up Jennifer, arriving in Daytona (all in less than 72 hours) was brutal, but it was worth it. I was 19 years old in that picture. The Hurst people could not have been more attentive, accommodating, and fun."

Jack Duffy liked to shoot photos of me for promotional reasons, such as these when I was relaxing by the pool on our way to Hawaii for an Armed Forces show.

Jack Duffy and Booper about to drive me around Daytona during the 500. What a ride. We started in 1966 with a Chrysler 300H, then had a Pontiac Grand Prix in 1968 and 1969, and eventually had the Oldsmobile pace car from 1972 to 1974. All of them had the same big gold shifter handle. That shifter is now in the fabulous Speedway Automotive Museum in Lincoln, Nebraska.

In contrast to the glamour of Daytona were local parades, such as this Christmas parade in Philadelphia. Mother made the costume, but it certainly didn't keep me warm. George about froze me to death!

At Daytona in my overalls. My daddy wore overalls so I did too, except mine hung a little differently than most.

I just loved the Hurst Olds cars. This is the 1974 with a big-block 455 HO engine, dual exhaust, and of course a Hurst shifter. This was the hardtop and we also had two convertibles for the parade cars. Those were fantastic cars. I still have the 1975 sitting in my garage, but unfortunately the 1974 isn't parked next to it. I love that outfit; wasn't I a pretty little thing? I'm trying to get my hair like that again, but that dress sure isn't going to fit anymore!

This was one of the convertible Hurst Olds Pace Cars. Notice the Hurst wheels too.

it now, although I have two attorneys trying to get me what's rightfully mine. He who stole my pension, and I'm pretty sure I know who he is even though I'm not going to mention names, but I'm sure he's going to rot downstairs with the devil. That was something I earned, working in the elements, standing with blisters on my feet, traveling with earaches. I got the job done and I only want what's rightfully mine. George Hurst would turn over in his grave if he knew I didn't have it.

I still have attorneys working to get my pension and I'm not giving up. I paid it in, each company paid it in half-and-half, and I'm due my money. I want to leave it for my family.

As Miss Hurst Golden Shifter, I used to do speed shop openings, and I always tried to model one of the shop's T-shirts. This was from Bailey Brothers Speed Shop in American Canyon, California. Fred and Sam Bailey had a respected engine building shop that concentrated on engines for sprint cars and drag racers. (Photo Courtesy Fred Bailey)

Jack Duffy and I at the NHRA U.S. Nationals in 1972 with one of our Hurst Oldsmobiles and the Hurst trailer in the background. (John Hilger Photo)

This was at the U.S. Nationals by the Hurst Aid trailers. Mother made that outfit. Boy didn't I have a figure back then? I'm saying to the little boy, "Make sure your daddy puts a Hurst shifter in his car, and quit looking up my dress!" (Photo Courtesy Mike Mikulice)

One of the things we would do at the trade and car shows was set up demonstrations with the products, where you could sit and row the gears on a Hurst shifter. This was at the 1970 SEMA show, when we won Best New Product for the Saf-T-Trigger shifter. I think that's Jerry Hatch, who worked with Hurst, in the chair shifting gears, and Bob Airheart is in the background with the sideburns. (Bob McClurg Photo)

I loved this car and Mother made the outfit.

In addition to the races I did as Miss Hurst Golden Shifter, we did a lot of appearances and promotions at car shows and other events. This was at the Hot Rod Supernationals at Englishtown, New Jersey. (Photo Courtesy Todd Wingerter)

At every drag race, I'd be on the big Hurst Golden Shifter and we'd make a parade lap. We did all of the NHRA races during the year so I spent a lot of time up on that platform holding the Hurst Shifter. (Photo Courtesy Todd Wingerter)

This was taken at an Armed Forces show, with George Bignotti (in the glasses behind me) and Al Unser Sr. next to me. Al took part in a lot of our Armed Forces shows.

Hurst also manufactured automatic shifters, including the very successful Dual/Gate as seen in this Hot Rod magazine ad from June 1969. That's Marsha Bennett and Super Stock racer Don Grotheer on the left, and me with Dickey Harrell on the right. (Photo Courtesy Hurst)

Gino Ballino! My famous friend who played at the Hurst party for us. Gino was one of the best sax players I ever met, besides Bobby Keys from the Rolling Stones. I had this thing for saxophone players. On the left is one of our Hurst guys who brought the Hurst SC/Rambler down to Daytona for George Hurst.

Showing a customer my Hurst shifter at the SEMA Show in 1968.

Look at that body! Where did that body go? Bring it back! Mother made the outfit and said, "What are you doing with fishnet?" I said, "Catching men, Mother!"

The ever-handsome James Garner and I.

My two Hurst Oldsmobiles in my driveway at home. The black one is a 1979 and the white one, a 1975, the last car that George Hurst did before he passed away and the last 455 big-block. That's Big Beauty.

My return to the Indianapolis Motor Speedway with Jack "Doc" Watson for the Hurst Olds Club of America. And what does it do that day? It rains. But we did a parade lap and bowed just like we always did anyway. Jack and I made magic together, putting together all kinds of promotions. He just passed away recently, God rest his soul. I really miss him.

Courtney Hansen

// Linda Vaughn is like family to me. My dad, Jerry Hansen, raced in the SCCA circuit, and owned Brainerd International Raceway in Minnesota, so I grew up at the racetracks. Linda was always at the races and of course is an icon in that world. As a little girl I admired her, loved her elaborate gold and white costumes, and found her to be such a natural beauty. My dad always said that, besides my mom, Linda was the most gorgeous woman he had ever seen in person.

"After beginning work in automotive TV in my 20s I attended SEMA and the Barrett-Jackson auctions every year, and of course I always saw Linda. I don't think there is an automotive event that she misses. In spite of the long lines at her appearance sessions she would welcome me over for a quick hello and hug. We would catch up for a few minutes when there was a chance. One time at Barrett-Jackson she got on the phone to say hello to my Dad, which meant the world to him.

"Several years ago Chevrolet Performance hired us to do autograph signings at the big car shows across the country. What an honor it was to be asked to sign posters alongside Linda Vaughn! From the Detroit Autorama and the Woodward Dream Cruise to the NHRA Nationals and Hot Rod Power Tour, we traveled the country hanging with fans and having a blast together. We became like sisters without any drama or competitive energy between us. We have always supported each other and built each other up.

"Nobody makes me laugh as hard as Linda. She is incredibly witty with one-liners for days, and there is continuous laughter, whether working or playing. At autograph signings she has me and everyone in the lines cracking up. The fans just love it. Linda has tremendous charisma and personality. She is constant entertainment.

"After becoming great friends on tour we started going to NASCAR, IndyCar, and GrandAM races together, and it's been special getting to know her on a more personal level. She introduced me to her dear friend Chip Ganassi, and there was a time we flew to multiple races in the same weekend. She took me to my first Indianapolis 500, which is an unforgettable memory.

"At the races and events Linda is always a star surrounded by adoring fans. I just love that she takes time to sign autographs and talk with every person, remembering her fans' names and the fun stories they share of the past. Linda is a true automotive enthusiast with so much knowledge and passion.

"She doesn't just attend the Sunday race. She goes to the qualifying sessions and all of the races. She can talk cars and racing all day long, and she has an amazing repertoire of stories. The way she recounts them and tells jokes is an art form she has mastered. "She also has a beautiful singing voice. At a restaurant in Detroit one night while listening to a pianist play, Linda sang throughout dinner.

"Linda is a very genuine, caring person. She always asks about my family and close friends, of course remembering everyone. No matter how busy she is, she makes time for me. She's extremely thoughtful, always giving meaningful gifts and sending sweet notes. She offers wonderful advice and has been a loving, supportive friend over the years.

"NASCAR champion Tony Stewart probably sums it up best. Whenever he sees us at the tracks he says, "Here comes double trouble." Linda is an icon who paved the way for women to be embraced in the automotive space. She is beautiful inside and out. She is a legend. I am proud to call her my friend."

If I had my pension I wouldn't have to be working as hard as I do now. Everyone thinks I have it made but I try to take care of my sisters in Georgia, and I buy nice things for the family when I can and I keep my head above water, but I'm still having to work too hard. I need to slow down for my own health. I've been a little sick recently and it irritates me when I get sick but it's the fans who keep me going. Of course if I drank and raised hell I'd probably not be sick but I'm not a drinker, I'm a worker. I love PR and marketing and advertising, NHRA, IndyCar, NASCAR, the auctions, car shows. It's a real honor getting to work with our guys.

I've never had very many girlfriends in my life because they wouldn't understand. But Booper and my mother, they understood. And so did June Cochran and most of my Hurstettes.

I love this picture of Courtney Hansen and I, signing our Camaro posters at Steve Plunkett's Fleetwood in London, Ontario, Canada. I was dressed like a little schoolgirl.

" Back in the '60s and '70s, Linda Vaughn was the girl of every boy's dreams. I finally met her about 20 years ago in the early days of my television show, *My Classic Car,* and we've been friends ever since. That's probably not uncommon though. I don't think Linda has met many people that weren't friends. She is possibly the most pleasant, charming, and genuinely likeable person I have ever known. It's not an act either. That's just who she is. She has an uncanny ability to make everyone she meets feel special.

"Our paths have crossed many times over the years, and I've gotten to know her fairly well. She is a delight to be around and believe me, she has some great stories! Linda is an icon, and there will never be another like here. She's still the girl of my dreams! "

— Dennis Gage

Here we are at same show. I'm sitting on TV personality Dennis Gage's knee, with Courtney sitting next to Steve Plunkett. He puts on a great show as a fundraiser and gets thousands of cars there.

Hurst Advertising

These are just some of the magazine advertisements we did at Hurst, showing all the different products we offered. The chassis-based ad showed how we had a car covered nearly from nose to tail with high-performance products, and of course my mother made the uniform again, but check out my chassis!

The Build a Better Bug showed what we had for the red-hot Volkswagen scene in the 1960s and 1970s, with shifters, a clutch, and shock absorbers. Everybody laughed at us when we came out with the VW line, but the worst thing in an old Bug is the shifter, so we built one, it worked, and we sold millions and millions of them. So who was laughing then?

The only thing I didn't like about this timeframe at Hurst was when they bought the shock company. I liked everything else but just didn't care for the shocks. The Schiefer Clutches, Trigger shifters, Airheart brakes were all fantastic, but I thought the shocks were a pain in the butt and a waste of money, and I told it like it was. In the end, it cost the company money; it didn't make it any. (Photos Courtesy Hurst)

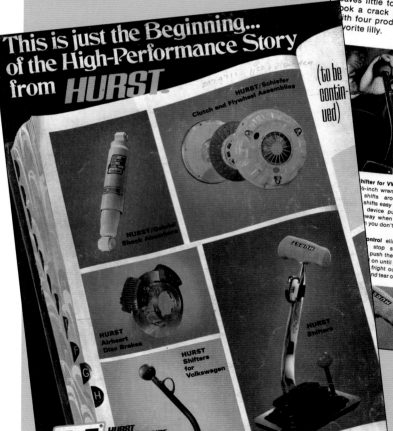

The Hurst Armed Forces Club

George Hurst and Jack Duffy had both retired from the navy (one of my nicknames for George was Gorgeous George from Valley Forge), so they loved the military and would do anything they could for them. At Hurst headquarters, there was a navy/air force base right up the street, and George would hire the veterans from the base. We had some great navy engineers at Hurst, and George would hire the hand-icapped guys as well; we had blind people running our cafeteria and they made great food, and other handicapped folks ran the back of the shop and kept it clean. George was a great philanthropist and a great believer in the armed forces, and out of that came the Hurst Armed Forces Club.

The club was less about promoting the Hurst name than it was giving back to the soldiers and give them a good time. We published the *Hurst Armed Forces* newsletter and went all around the world to military bases and put on shows; we did radio and television spots, special dinners, special assignments; we ran contests and we visited the hospitals too. A lot of times when it was close to home, we would take Bob Riggle and the Hurst *Hemi Under Glass* and make exhibition runs, and of course I was there with my Hurstettes. I think the boys really appreciated the whole thing.

We also went all over the world to military bases, including a few trips to Vietnam, and on those tours we got to know Generals Curtis LeMay and General Olbert F. Lassiter. I actually met the Generals through Jimmy Clark when he ran the Indianapolis 500. They were great friends with Jimmy, and I just found them so

We made up this banner for the Hurst Armed Forces Club and gave them out wherever we could. This photo was taken at our hotel in Hawaii before a show at a base there.

wonderful to talk with and spend time with, and I was so proud that Jimmy introduced me. As the years went by I ran into General LeMay quite often and I stayed in touch with General Lassiter.

As a matter of fact, General Lassiter, chief of the U.S. Air Force Command Post, Head-quarters U.S. Air Force, gave me a 15-karat diamond ring and asked me to marry him, but he was too old for me. I was only 19 and I had to turn him down because my career had just started and I had a lot to do. I wanted to explore my own chances and build my own name. My mother said she'd marry him though! I was very honored and flattered, but I did not want to get married. Are you kidding me?! I waited until I was 30 to even try it, and that's unheard of in Georgia; if you're not mar-ried by 16, you're an old maid! I'm an old maid again so I love it. But it sure was fun. When I was dating the General, we'd fly in on a private

*At an Armed Forces Naval base with the Hurst **Hemi Under Glass** and Bob Riggle. Bob was a brilliant guy. We did those Armed Forces shows on and off forever.*

The Hurst Armed Forces Club *CONTINUED*

This is with Bob Riggle and the Hurst Hemi Under Glass aboard one of the navy ships, I think the USS Enterprise. We'd sign pictures on top of the car for the sailors and take pictures, and Bob would pick the wheels up a couple of times on the deck of the ship.

Lear jet and land at Valley Forge and out stepped three- and four-star Generals and me, and George would pick us up. What a sight that must have been.

Bob Hope was doing his USO shows at the same time, and the Generals got in touch with me to meet him back in the states, so I met them all in Beverly Hills and we had lunch. We discussed what I had been doing and Bob was enamored with my personality and how I handled the troops, and he invited me to a couple of his shows. I was so honored!

To just be in the presence of Bob Hope is something that I'll never forget. When I walked out on stage I had this red fringe outfit on and I'd say, "I don't sing and I don't dance, but I'll sure shift your gears!" And everybody would hoot and holler.

Bob Hope later sent me a gold cigarette lighter with his nose on it. Knowing that I don't smoke, he said, "Light your candles with this." I thought that was so cute, and I still have that gold lighter. It's a treasure.

As I said I went all over the world with the Generals and Bob Hope, Jimmy Stewart, Ed McMahon. They were all a part of their own little Air Force and it was a wonderful experience.

Then there were the astronauts! They were stationed at Cape Canaveral, which isn't that far from Daytona, so they used to come up to all the tests, like the tire tests we did for Goodyear. They all had Corvettes with Hurst shifters in them, and Mr. France would give us hot tips when they were coming so we got to know them all.

During our Armed Forces Club tours, we would do the ground shows and the Blue Angels would do the air shows. George Hurst was great friends with Capt. Bob Aumack and the guys and made me Miss Navy this year, so I got to go on a ride with the Blue Angels. Capt. Aumack, Lt. Cmdr. Wheat, Hubbard . . . they were all just the best and these guys were gorgeous, God-fearing guys.

I'll never forget one night though, we were up at Los Alamitos Naval Air Station and we all went to dinner and the bar, and they were drinking Courvoisier. That stuff will kill you just smelling it, but they were downing them like water. I thought, "How the hell are they going to fly the next day?" But as soon as they'd hit their oxygen they were like brand new. George sure had a hangover the next day, though!

Captain Bob made arrangements and I went to Willow Grove NAS in Pennsylvania and flew with them. Of course, I threw up all over the cockpit. They said, "If you don't throw up, you're not a pilot." I'd never do it again, but I'm glad I got to fly with them. It scared the hell out of me, especially when they pulled the stick; it's not fun to puke in your face mask. You go straight up, then straight back down, then they do it again.

I think my boobs shrank that day because I was holding it in, pushing it out, holding it in. They thought I was cool, but it scared the hell out of me.

I was one of their pals. That was so great because they respected me and I respected them, and I would go watch the launches; we were very close. A lot of people probably don't realize that our industry made a lot of things for NASA and NASA made a lot of things for the automotive industry, and I was involved in all the marketing and public relations things.

All of the original astronauts were lovely people. Pete Conrad was my neighbor here in Southern California until he got killed on a motorcycle on Pacific Coast Highway not far from my house. A lot of the guys would come to the Indianapolis 500 every year. I didn't know Neil Armstrong very well (he was a very nice but quiet man), but my roommate did.

Gordon Cooper and Pete Conrad were the two crazies of the group. One time, they decided to come see me in Georgia on the way to somewhere and they flew in with a T-33 and landed at Chattanooga. We took an old drag 'chute and covered the plane (like we were going to get away with it!) and all went out.

We went up to Ellis's to eat and of course they had to try the white lightning. They couldn't get out of Dalton, Georgia, without trying some moonshine; I mean that's all there was too it! So we went to my brother's house. I called and told C. B. I was bringing some friends and he said, "Who you got comin'?"

I said, "You won't believe me if I tell you."

He said, "Well, who is it?"

I said, "A couple of astronauts."

And he says, "Yeah sure."

So I didn't say anything else and when they got there, the look on my brother's face was like "Hooooly crap, it's the astronauts! Here, have a drink! Shake the bead on it we'll see how much bead's on there."

I'll never forget when Pete Conrad said to C. B., "Hell we could fly on this stuff. We can pour this in the tank and fly out of here."

I have to say I think they both really liked it! I couldn't drink that stuff but Booper drank with them and they were really funny. I wish I could have recorded that night. I mean, we got world-renowned astronauts slipping in to see us, and we hid them out good. Those guys were rock stars, and so were we that night!

That was fun, hiding the astronauts. Later on, C. B. said, "Don't go back to the airport, there's a bunch of media out there," so Booper and I put them in taxis and sent them back to the airport.

We had a great rapport with the armed forces and I spent a lot of time with these great Generals. They told me what to watch out for, told me exactly what was going to happen. All about the terrorists, what to watch out for, and boy were they right. I think I got a PhD in what they were talking about and it's both amazing and frightening.

I'm glad I don't have any children because right now I'd be frightened to death to have a child the way things are going. I don't let my guard down. I have to lock my

This was a highlight night of my life, when my dear friend Bob Hope surprised me by presenting my award at the SEMA Hall of Fame, thanks to the great Dick Wells, who set it up. It was so wonderful and I was delighted and so proud. Thank you Dick Wells. That was a gold and copper dress, Miss Hurst Golden Shifter's colors. Wow, look at that figure; I wish I looked like that now.

My Vietnam boys, I loved them all. We'd send them cutouts when we couldn't be there, and they would often send us letters and photographs back posing with them, like these guys in a tank crew.

doors at night and turn on my alarm, and we never even locked our doors in Georgia, you know? You have to watch and make sure nobody's following you on the way home in one of your muscle cars because it invites trouble. It's a pretty troubled world we live in, so band together Americans!

Some Jersey boys ran some promotional races down in Puerto Rico so we went with Hurst and Hemi Under Glass. This is Bob Riggle, George Hurst, the track promoter (who didn't speak English), Billy Ostrove, and me.

J. C. Penney was a big sponsor because we sold our products there and they had all these dignitaries there that had never seen a drag race in their lives. It was a lot of fun. I was rushed after we ran the car when they knocked the fence over, and this one guy grabbed me. Never in my entire career did I ever hit but one person. I told this guy "no touchy" and he grabbed me and I popped him one and he got the message. By the time George and Bob got to him, I'd already knocked him out. One punch and I laid him out!

I had so much fun I stayed a whole 10 days down there with Billy after the race and went water skiing, mountain climbing, all kinds of fun things. I loved being with Billy; he was a sweetheart and it was a blast.

That's Hayden Proffitt, The Rebel, and I on our Armed Forces tour in Hawaii at the Tripler Army Medical Center. We did the show outside and cranked the cars up, then we went inside the hospital and visited all the soldiers. These guys, some of them amputees, hadn't seen a girl except for their nurses for months, and this one guy had a tent over his foot because it was so badly injured, and Hayden said, "Are you just glad to see Linda or did you build her that tent?"

I slapped him and said, "You crazy thing!" He was just always laughing and was great with the guys there. Hayden was a real character and I was always happy to work with him. George Hurst was close with all the American Motors people, and Al Carpenter put together this whole promotion for American Motors and we did the Javelins and the funny cars, Trans Am cars; we were all a big happy family and Hayden Proffitt was a part of it. He's still kickin' and still fishin'.

Outside Tripler Army Medical Center in Hawaii, visiting our wounded warriors. That's Lila Hurst, George's wife, on the left. She was a great cook and had the best personality; and the prettiest legs. I was so proud of her and George; we really had a great family and I was always so proud to go to any event with them. Lila wasn't the jealous type. She loved me for my personality and my hard work. And her daughter, George's step daughter, became my friend and we put them all in costumes and worked a lot of events together.

Here "I" am with one of my soldier boys in Vietnam. We had 50,000 names on our mailing list and sent a lot of those cutouts over there.

A part of the Armed Forces Club was holding contests and promotions and things, and choosing a soldier to come to the races with us and ride with me in the pace car. This was a navy boy riding with me at the drag races in Pomona.

On the left is saxophone player Geno Bellino talking to my brother C. B. during an Armed Forces day at Daytona. Everybody thought C. B. was Carroll Shelby because they looked a lot alike. That's Booper next to C. B. and his wife Pat next to her. What a crowd there was that day.

At the NHRA U.S. Nationals in Indianapolis in 2015, our guest was this gentleman, the oldest decorated World War II veteran we still have. He wanted a picture with me, and it was my honor to pose with him.

I was at Indianapolis on pit lane right before the start of the race, and army General Vaughn walked by with two of his boys so we took this picture. I call General Vaughn my kissin' cousin! And those guys in back are my Indiana State Police boys. I have one of their hats.

As part of the Hurst Armed Forces promotion, an artist in Pennsylvania built this little model Jeep for George.

3 THE HURSTETTES

The job of Miss Hurst Golden Shifter was far more than a full-time affair; I was traveling constantly, not just around the country but around the world too. With 134 events in a year, I was working so hard that after a couple of years it became apparent that I needed some help.

There could only be one Miss Hurst Golden Shifter: That was me, and I had worked very hard to make it what it is. But I thought if I could develop some helpers and call them the Hurstettes, it would allow us to be in multiple places at once. We could still maintain the brand of Miss Hurst because we had made it so popular, iconic even.

For example, if I had to open a warehouse or attend an event on the East Coast, I could send a Hurstette to a function in the Midwest or West Coast. But I had worked so hard to build up the name and the Hurst brand, that to have some trashy woman come in here and screw it up would be wrong.

Patty Flannery wasn't the only Miss Hurst before me; George had put several, shall we say, less-than-professional, women on that shifter before me. I built my name and brand and I protected it like a lioness mother does her cubs, so we couldn't have just any model working with us.

We came up with the "Hurstettes." The first was June Cochran, a tiny blonde who I called Junebug. So next, I picked Nikki Phillips, a tall brunette beauty, and then Shelley Harmon Bell, who had legs up to her armpits. They all came onboard in the span of about a year; after that I had maybe seven or eight Hurstettes over the years.

I only hired girls who could do the job, and I snapped the whip. I had a training program to take them out and see how they acted around people and at events, and we had a lot of meetings. We were representing the Hurst brand, which George, Jack Duffy, and I had worked our butts off to make it the household name that it was. They were held to a very high standard, but we still had a lot of fun!

That's me in the middle, flanked by Hurstettes Marsha Bennett (left) and Nikki Phillips (right). Talk about a triple threat.

That's me on the shifter, Junebug looking the other direction and Shelley Harmon Bell between us. They were both beautiful girls and I was so proud of them.

June Cochran

I think it was a subconscious thought at first. I knew I needed some help with so many events, but I hadn't really put it all together in my head until we were at the *Hot Rod* drags at Riverside Raceway in California. I had met the *Playboy* Playmate of the Year, June Cochran, earlier at Indianapolis and just fell in love with her, so I brought her to Riverside for the race and introduced her to George.

She was such a dear, sweet little fan, and the most gorgeous, tiny thing you'd ever seen. She became my second-best friend and Booper just loved her too.

I sat down with George at Riverside and told him what I was thinking and that this could be a great opportunity for us. I drew up a rendering of what the group would look like, costumes and all. I told him that I wanted June to be my Hurstette and he thought it was a great idea. She was a natural for the job because, for one, she was incredibly beautiful, and for two, she was very personable and she knew how to be professional from the *Playboy* experience. I knew I could send her out to an event and she would do the job right, not sleep around, or do something stupid. And of course everybody just loved Junebug.

From left to right are Marsha Bennett, June Cochran, Nikki Phillips, and me, holding court on the starting line. I had a golf cart with a Hurst shifter on it. That's Nikki and Marsha looking off in the distance and Junebug discussing race strategy with me.

June and I riding the Hurst Shifter and goofing off. I'm pretty sure this was at the Pocono IndyCar race and we were picking on and mouthing off to A. J. Foyt, which we did a lot because we were good at that!

June "Junebug" Cochran was my first Hurstette. She was Playboy's Playmate of the Year and I invited her to the Hot Rod magazine drag race at Riverside International Raceway in Riverside, California. This photo is from that day, when I convinced George to hire her and make her a Hurstette. We put her in black and gold right after that. Junebug was so beautiful, so pretty. I just loved her to pieces. She went on to get married and have a couple of boys, and sadly died of diabetes. But her death saved my life because it forced me to get checked for diabetes, and I found out I have it too. So in a sense, Junebug saved my life. (Bob McClurg Photos)

"I really enjoyed watching Linda; how she handled herself around other people and the way she made everybody just feel good about what they were doing was just amazing."

Marsha Bennett had the most beautiful legs, a gorgeous face, and she had a real movie-star quality, lovely personality, kind of shy and quiet. She sure got the attention of the Mazmanian group, and Richard Siroonian. I thought he wanted to marry her; it was hilarious. I've never seen anybody flip over anybody the way they did over Marsha. But it was such a great family, all of us. She was Miss California and Nikki was a Miss USA runner-up, so I had some real beauties.

Marsha Bennett

Marsha was actually discovered by Jack Duffy. He asked me what I thought, and I said, "Oh yes." She had the most beautiful smile and was so lovely (she looked like Princess Grace) and had the most gorgeous legs. Marsha was very sweet, very kind, and just lovely. I'm not the jealous type but she was one of the most beautiful girls I ever hired. Kind of quiet but she did her job very well and people fell in love with her. They say a picture's worth 1,000 words and one look, that's all it took. She didn't work with us very long but she sure was pretty.

Thoughts from Marsha:

"After working in photography modeling for a few years, I was fortunate to become Miss California. I was asked to be a part of a USO tour with Johnny Grant to support our troops in Vietnam. Being with the troops in a war zone was the most moving experience of my life. It was a tremendous honor to be able to bring a little joy and a little touch of home to our soldiers in the field and to share a smile and exchange a kind word with the wounded men in the hospitals. My heart was so full of emotion, great happiness, and deep sorrow, but always extreme pride in those young men. As I write this today, these emotions swell my heart and fill my eyes with tears, trying to express the honor I felt in being a part of this.

"In contrast, a while after returning home I was asked to participate in a very fun event as Miss Winternationals. It was my first time at the drag races. It was great fun! While I was there, I was introduced to the Hurst representatives and they asked if I would work with them, primarily on the West Coast. Being new to the racing world, as I had grown up in the world of sports such as golf, tennis, boating, etc., I did not know of Linda, yet.

"Of course everyone had a lot to say about her and they were such wonderful things. I finally was able to meet Linda for myself when I went to a few of the big races in the East. Yes, she was a delight to work with and to be around. She was warm and charm-

Here I am with Marsha Bennett.

ing, but more than that, she was brilliant, so brilliant that she sparkled, with her eyes, with her smile, with her total being.

"I had a wonderful time working with Linda. The entire Hurst Family were all extremely caring and the height of professionalism. To say that I had a terrific time and have marvelous memories of Linda and the Hurst Company would be an understatement. It was wonderful!"

Shelley Harmon

Shelley Harmon was precious. I called her Maxine because she reminded me of the Maxine cartoon character with long skinny arms and big feet. Shelley was hard to find boots for because she had the biggest feet! I went all over Hollywood trying to find her boots, and when we finally found them I bought a whole bunch of them so we'd have plenty of good-looking boots and shoes for her.

I met her at the races when she was working for free, and took her up to get her some money, but I was really auditioning her. I liked the way she listened and learned with me, how poised she was and would stand and talk right. I hired her after that race. I could send Shelley to the store openings without worry because she had such a wonderful personality. What was special about Shelley was that she was a racer.

Shelley, June, and I traveled together the most and Mother loved and adopted them both. My mother called Shelley a "long drink of water" and I think my dad was a little sweet on her because of those legs, and Grumpy and everybody loved Shelley because of her personality. The three of us terrorized A. J. and Mario. It was our work and we enjoyed it.

When you enjoy your work and you're having fun, you make people smile. It was always entertaining, it was sports entertainment, and it was always classy. We were something else that's for sure, and a lot of folks still remember us!

This is me with another one of my Hurstettes, Shelley Harmon Bell. I always said that she had legs up to her armpits. Well, this dress proved that! Shelley was a fantastic Hurstette, and an even better friend.

"Linda and I hung out for the rest of those five days. She was a role model for me and I felt that I was in the presence of royalty!"

This was at the Daytona 500, one of our favorite races, with Shelley and I surrounding my mother. Remember, Mother made most of our outfits, so she was always an integral part of the entire Hurst deal.

Shelley Harmon Bell.

Thoughts from Shelley:

I have always loved cars and drag racing since I can remember. My dad built me a turquoise go-cart with a helmet to match and I raced with the boys when I was 6 years old. I was fearless and still am. At the age of 63, I ride my customized Harley Fat Boy and have been owning and riding motorcycles since I was 13.

My first boyfriend, Gary Ewing, raced a 1969 Super Stock 302 Z-28 called *Little Zipper* at the time. We would go to all the races around the Maryland, Pennsylvania, and New Jersey areas. Especially the 75-80 Dragway in Baltimore. It was a fast car and rarely lost a race. Gary let me drive sometimes. I learned from him how to cut a light and not red-light. I was 17 and a girl in 1970. It was unheard of when I beat the guys. Their morale was shattered.

A few months later the car and team (Gary Ewing and Brothers) was sponered by Schmitt's Beer Brewing Company in Pennsylvania. Schmitt's hired me as "Miss Schmitts Beer of Philadelphia" and I toured with the team to all the NHRA events and car shows as a model with the car.

In 1972, we were at the Summernationals and a official from NHRA approached me and asked me if I could please pose as Miss Summernationals. I couldn't believe it! I was so excited! Of course I said yes. And just then, up rolls Linda Vaughn on her golf cart. I knew who she was because she was an idol. She introduced herself to me in her Southern drawl and her personality was electic.

I told her that I was going to be Miss Summernationals. She says "Honey, how much are they paying you?"

I thought to myself "paying me? Is she crazy?" I was elated to volunteer and felt ecstatic just to be the Drag Queen at the NHRA Summernationals.

I told her that and she said, "Jump on the golf cart with me. We are going to get you paid!"

She rolled up to the NHRA headquarters and took me in. She asked, "How much are you going to pay Shelley for being your Queen?"" They looked astonished and said they would pay me $25.

"She said, "Forget it! You will pay her $100 a day!"

They bowed their heads and said, "Of course, Linda."

I was dying! $100 a day to do something I loved and would have done for free? That $100 today would be like making $600 per day. At that time,

Jim Kelly was a very well known and respected drag racing photographer and took a lot of pictures of the Hurstettes and me. This was on the starting line at the U.S. Nationals in Indianapolis and we were just chatting him up. We were probably saying, "Sure you can take our picture. We don't mind."

I had a weekly job as a receptionist in Baltimore, and I was being paid $40 a week for 45 hours!

Linda and I hung out for the rest of those five days. She was a role model for me and I felt that I was in the presence of royalty! Everyone knew her and she knew everyone. She could, and still does, remember everyone's name, their family's names, where they live, their pet's names, dates, places; she is incredible.

She has a gift of remembering every detail about people and always gives them cute nicknames. She called me Maxine! To this day I still don't know why.

Linda was a role model for me. I had good manners and some decorum, but she taught me so much more. I was on the shy side and I attribute to her my ability to talk to anyone with confidence and poise. She always had a good, funny, comeback and I learned and used that to my advantage to be able to talk to anyone with self assurance.

After that initial meeting at the Summernationals, I ran into her again at the Springnationals in California and it was there she asked me to work with her as a "Hurstette." I was thrilled! It was then, in 1972, that my high-life began with Linda. Almost 50 years later we are still sisters.

Nikki Phillips O'Neill

Thoughts from Nikki:

"I was in college when I first met Linda Vaughn. I was going to the University of Maryland and my father was in the air force. He had asked me to help our troops at the Bethesda Naval Hospital by handing out gifts and things, and Linda was there too, representing Hurst. We had a great time walking up and down the aisles and talking to the guys, trying to cheer them up. She asked me if I wanted to represent Hurst with her at some racing events and I thought, 'Sure, that sounds like a great idea; it might be fun.' So that's how we met.

"I needed a job to pay for my schooling the next year so I had a job over the summer, and I worked on weekends for Linda. I would finish my classes

Nikki and I kissing photographer Jim Kelly. He was such a sweetheart, and those gladiator boots I was wearing were famous!

I have always just loved this picture of Nikki (left), June (rear), and me. June was such a sweetheart and loved to have a lot of fun. We all did. (Tom McCrea Photo)

This is a really special photo. It's at the U.S. Nationals in Indy. Jack Duffy is driving and it's Marsha Bennett and Nikki on the back, with me on the shifter. We pulled out and we were looking good; all the Hurst cars assembled in one place, even the AMC SC/Rambler is back there. In the shot is one of the Hurst Olds convertibles, five H/O coupes, the SC/Rambler (which looked like a mailbox to me) and an S/S AMX bringing up the rear.

on a Friday and then on Friday night or Saturday morning get on a plane and go to a race. Then I'd come back Monday ready for classes.

"I had been dating my boyfriend, who has been my husband for 45 years now, for four years at the time and he didn't mind me going off to the races at all. He used to play rugby so he would be busy with sports stuff on the weekends and wasn't jealous at all. I won Miss DC in a televised contest with 50 women in 1970 that qualified me to go to the Miss USA contest in Miami Beach. I asked him, 'Are you going to watch?'

"He said, 'Yes, if we're not playing.' We were solid from the beginning. I got 7th runner-up in Miss USA, by the way.

"I started in 1968 and was involved with Linda and Hurst for more than 10 years. I'd go to some races by myself because Linda couldn't be everywhere at once, where there were multiple races going on, and Hurst wanted to have a presence. I had a great time; it was a great experience.

"Linda's an incredibly personable person, so what we'd do is go to the pits and walk around, she'd talk to the guys about their work, some of the technicalities about just racing in general. She was so fun and smiley and I was sort of her sidekick. We enjoyed subtly promoting Hurst, but everybody knew who she was. She was famous, and still is.

"I really enjoyed sort of being a fly on the wall a little bit because I didn't know a lot about racing. I enjoyed meeting the racers and their crews and

Nikki and I doing our thing in George's convertible. Look how pretty Nikki looks here. I was very proud of her just for how hard she worked and how professional she was, but she was also a very smart lady who was lovely to work with. She's married and lives in Maryland today.

understanding what they did, and enjoyed the genuine personalities I got to meet through Linda. Big Daddy is, of course, one of my favorites, and Grumpy Jenkins too. The racers were great, incredible people and smart! Jeez, to do what they did and innovate the way they did is just incredible.

"Oh, and Linda's mom made all the clothes! I never got to meet her but I'm sure she was a fine woman, and she was a great seamstress.

"I really enjoyed watching Linda; how she handled herself around other people and the way she made everybody just feel good about what they were doing was just amazing. She just brightened up people's day. It was never intimidating for me and we were friends; she was the boss for sure, but I never felt intimidated.

"I mean I was an air force brat and grew up all around the world with six kids in my family. I was the oldest so being around people was not intimidating at all. It was awesome though, to meet these famous racers, but they were just genuine people like you and me.

"I finally ended my time as a Hurstette when I was in graduate school and four months pregnant. I got my Masters degree and then my Doctorate (in plant pathology), and all along I was doing glasswork. Now I'm a full-time glass sculptor and just had my first solo show (see NikkiOneillGlass.com). Life got busy and for quite a while I hadn't gained any weight and I was still pretty, so I could have gone on a little further, but it wasn't in the cards.

"I don't follow racing much any more, but I think about it every once in a while. You know, it's not front-and-center in the media; I don't see it much in the papers or on the news. I mean you hear about the Indy 500 and NASCAR, but not drag racing.

"It's a microcosm of people who are passionate about their work, but you don't see them. I've been involved in different aspects of that through the years, just sampling different types of life. I was involved with the National Geographic Society for a month on a trip; I felt like an observer but it was pretty cool.

"We took *White Mist*, a 61-foot yawl with Dr. Melville Bell Grosvenor who was the president of National Geographic. We took it from Gibson Island in Maryland all the way up the Hudson River and through the St. Lawrence Seaway into Nova Scotia. We were the crew, nine of us along with Grosvenor,

I really enjoyed watching Linda; how she handled herself around other people and the way she made everybody just feel good about what they were doing was just amazing.

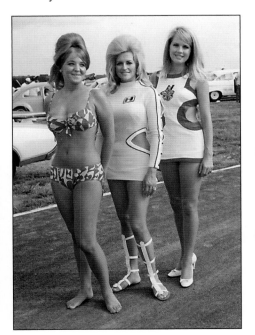

Miss Atlanta 500, me, and Nikki Phillips.

Tami Pittman was always running around the track, as part of her father K. S. Pittman's team. She and Leigh Buttera were two terrorizing little kids!

I figured I needed a Hurstette for the younger generation and when Tami really developed I thought she would be good, and she was. She grew up around racing so she knew it, and I like the girls that are into racing. I could get more work out of them and they'd work harder.

Tami was very good with people and her daddy was wonderful in that he trusted me with his daughter and let her travel with us. I had to keep an eye on her though; I was her chaperone! Her dad bought her a Boss 429 Mustang and she had the biggest crush on that car. I did too. She was a cute little thing. (Photo Courtesy Tami Pittman)

his wife, and son, plus an editor and a couple of photographers. I think I was just eye candy, but we were the crew and there are five pictures of me in that *National Geographic* issue. It was the cover story for July 1970, called 'North Through History Aboard *White Mist.*'

"We learned about the Revolutionary War history of the Hudson and had some interesting activities along the way, going to West Point and to Lawrence Rockefeller's estate for a stop over."

Tami Pittman

This looks like the drag races at Pomona, with Miss Pepperdine University, me, and Tami Pittman (racer K. S. Pittman's daughter). (Bob McClurg Photo)

Thoughts from Tami:

"Working with Linda Vaughn was nothing less than an honor. Linda is considered the First Lady of Racing. To me, a wonderful mentor. Being the youngest of the girls, Linda looked out for me, and always had my back. Although life has taken us in different directions and we have not been in touch for years, I still consider her a sister.

"I have so many wonderful memories of my time with Hurst and Linda. Being the daughter of a race car driver [K. S. Pittman], I grew up at the drags. So when Linda said we were going to the Indy 500, I was so excited. What an experience! Very different from anything I had ever experienced, more sophisticated and formal. What could have been better?

"Linda had me picked up at the airport by June Cochran and Mario Andretti. The entire week was filled with festivities and first-time experiences. Hurst had the Official Pace Car and we made the starting lap around the track waving at all the fans. I met the legends, and was a part of history.

"As much fun as we had, it was imperative that we always carry ourselves in a professional manner. We were more than beauty queens; we represented Hurst Performance. Linda made sure that all the girls were always treated with respect. If anyone was out of line, they would have to answer to Linda.

"I have a tremendous amount of respect for Linda. I learned so much from her and will be forever grateful for the wonderful experiences we shared. Linda brought so much beauty to the sport of auto racing and is a legend in her own right. Thank you, Linda Vaughn."

Sexism and Professionalism

If you weren't around in the 1960s, you might not know what the times were like for women, and women's rights. The efforts of women such as Gloria Steinam and others helped build the rise of feminism and it was The War of the Sexes for many people. And here we were, attractive models with

That's George Hurst's step-daughter Pam in the middle, with Booper (left) and my cousin Billie at Daytona. I put them to work, even Booper. Do you like that nice Hurst Oldsmobile in the background?

My sister-in-law Pat Vaughn at her first 500 in 1967, and my Hurstette Jackie from Nassau, Bahamas. I saw Jackie walking down the beach with a bunch of fruit on her head. She was a real native and turned out to be a real racing girl.

Photographer Bob McClurg flanked by two of my Hurstettes, my sister Sheila Ann Jeffcoat (left, who was going with Bob at the time) and my cousin Billie (right). (Bob McClurg Photo)

George Hurst and Jack Duffy ran some great promotions, and this was one of them. Hurst bought this Chevrolet Nova and fixed it up with their Hurst-A-Matic shifter and then gave it away as a promotion at the U.S. Nationals in Indianapolis. Walt Trapnell put his son's name on the ticket and he "won" the car. His son, Todd, really liked me! Nikki Phillips shot these photos of the giveaway in the Hurst Compound behind the tower. (Photos Courtesy Todd Trapnell)

" The car had several thousand miles on it because they drove to the various races promoting the contest. Hurst and Linda were very accommodating and our family enjoyed the trip immensely. When we were at Indy Linda taught Todd to say, 'super good' and to raise his hands with the peace sign (V) for Victory. Linda also brought Todd up to the podium at the Car Craft Banquet and upon returning him to our table he told his mother 'Mommy, she is soft'. "

— Walt Trapnell,
Todd's Dad

Nikki Phillips.

short skirts and lots of "natural talent" in a very male-dominated sport, so we got some attention from the feminists. Behind the scenes, women were very much a part of racing, especially when you think about the racers' wives who were an integral part of their team. Man or woman, we were one big family and we protected each other, and stood up for each other.

One time, a writer from New York City came down to Daytona to do a story, I think with an agenda to do a scandalous piece on women in racing. But she never went through the proper channels to get credentials for the race and pits. She just stormed in and demanded access, and when she was turned away (like anyone without credentials or the last name of France would be), she raised hell and screamed, "I'll sue them for defamation of character because I'm here to do a job!"

I cornered her and said, "You don't have to sue anyone. Why don't you just shut up and listen. The proper way to do it is to respectfully send a letter to Mr. Bill France Sr. and get the right credentials, and not come in here like some Yankee bitch trying to make a name for herself." Because that's what she was doing. I told her she would not get anywhere with these fine folks by acting that way.

"Number one, you're a Yankee and this is still the war-between-the-states down here. I accept you, but they will *not* accept you acting that way. Don't come in here and slap a lawsuit on every Tom, Dick, and Harry in the pits. That don't belong here. You have to *earn* the privilege of being in the pits. You're a writer, so write a letter, get your credentials set up properly, and treat us with respect because this is *our* industry, not yours."

Shelley, me and Junebug at the U.S. Nationals in Indianapolis. Look closely at the outfits. They had NHRA bed sheets with little dragsters and things on them, so Mother took them off the sheets and sewed them onto our outfits for some of the races. Wasn't that such a cute idea? (Bob McClurg Photo)

This was a really great day at Indianapolis Motor Speedway, with George Hurst, June Cochran, James Garner, and myself. We were doing a safety show using the Hurst Rescue Tool, which George Hurst invented.

Not a lot of people outside of racing know that George Hurst developed the Jaws of Life that you see first-responders use to get people out of badly crashed cars, and save their lives. George was a brilliant, brilliant man and a great engineer, but most of all he liked to help people and he loved increasing safety efforts wherever he could.

Hurst's Mr. Mancheski had been in a terrible automobile crash, and if he had had something to pull him out of the car quicker he wouldn't have lost his leg and some fingers, so that prompted George to invent his Rescue Tool, and the rest is history.

This photo was at the press conference at the hotel in Indianapolis for the unveiling of the Rescue Tool. George, June, and I went out shopping to get dressed up in bright orange outfits for safety: I cut the long pants off and made them short for June and me. Garner was there for the unveiling and we invited 2,500 fire chiefs from all over America for the debut.

This was also the day that Bill Simpson famously set himself on fire in front of everybody to show off his fireproof driving suit, but he didn't warn me that he was going to do it and I about had a heart attack!

This was at the 24 Hours of Daytona, with Bob Tullius talking to us at the fence. On the left is Jackie Hart Adams, my Hurstette from the Bahamas, and George Hurst's step-daughter Pam Hurst. Bob Tullius ran one of the most successful road racing teams from the 1960s through the 1980s, called Group 44 Inc. They raced in SCCA Club Racing, the IMSA GTO endurance events, and SCCA Trans-Am. I think he won the Trams-Am race in a Dodge Dart at Daytona, where this photo was taken. If you look close you can see the Hurst SC/Rambler shirts we're wearing.

People like that don't realize what life in the tight-knit racing world is like. You can have breakfast with someone in the morning and you might be going to the funeral home that night. Racing is serious business, and I told her, "Don't **** with it!" That's exactly what I said to her.

Other than that one instance, we didn't really have many problems with the whole feminist crowd. They tried to portray me one way, but I never burned my bra! There was one time at the New York Auto Show. George Hurst had just come out with a new Hurst shifter and I was talking about it on the turntable, and we had the Smothers Brothers with us too, and some woman started giving me crap about it, basically saying I was nothing more than a bimbo.

I fired back, "Well honey, this bimbo can talk about cars. What are you doing here? You're doing a story? Do you know what you're talking about when it comes to cars? Do you know what kind of engine this car has, what kind of transmission?" That shut her up.

I was making an intelligent speech about the car on the turntable, and I wouldn't stand for anyone insulting my intelligence. I was only 26 at the time but I did my homework and I could talk cars with the best of 'em. Some women saw me as a bimbo until I spoke.

All I can say is, don't judge a book by its cover. You gotta read the contents.

> 66 Linda was always the consummate professional and represented Hurst and racing well. She was a fixture at the track and always created a lot of excitement wherever she went. She did her job very well; a beautiful woman and always a lady. 99
>
> — Bob Tullius

Patty and Jackie, "The Bahama Mama," with the Hurst SC/Rambler, and me behind the steering wheel. We were doing a Hurst SC/Rambler promotion at this race. I didn't particularly like driving that little SC/Rambler, but one time out in the parking lot we lined up a couple of them and I put a Coca Cola can in front of one and I jumped over it in first gear! Not to offend any of you SC/Rambler guys but it looked like a mailbox (we called it the U.S. Mail Machine) but it would hop and jump, I'll tell you that!

In the winner's circle at Riverside Raceway in California after the Hot Rod Magazine Championship Drag Races. That's Hot Rod publisher Ray Brock on the left and Dandy Dick Landy on the right, after "Dimples" (as I called Landy) had won a race.

Dick Landy was another brother in racing, and Ray Brock was for sure a big ol' brother of mine too. Brock and George Hurst were the best of friends. I don't think they could out-drink each other, but they surely could most other men. I don't know how they made it through racing the next day. Dimples: That boy could shift some gears and he could drive, drive, drive!

Dick and his wife, Gean, were my friends right up until his passing in 2007, and I just saw her not long ago. I was also very close to Ray Brock, his wife Joanne, and his kids. He would have Christmas parties and have everyone over, including Parnelli Jones and his kids. Brock was a real man's man; that is probably why he and George Hurst got along so well.

THE WORLD OF DRAG RACING

Because you're reading this book, there's a better than average chance that you know the history of drag racing, and specifically the birth of the NHRA. If you don't, please allow for a brief history lesson.

NHRA Formation

Wally Parks, from Oklahoma, served in the South Pacific during World War II, and like many young men returning from war, got into hot rods. Specifically, running hot rods on the dry lakes in Southern California. Top speed was all that mattered on the lakes. Wally was one of the instrumental people who helped form the Southern California Timing Association (SCTA) in 1947. Dry lakes racers had a place to compete against one another; the deciding factor was the timing equipment that showed the legitimate speeds that the hot rods had achieved.

Two years later, the SCTA held its first race on the famed Bonneville Salt Flats in Utah. Not long after that, C. J. "Pappy" Hart adapted "computerized" timing equipment to a makeshift quarter-mile drag strip on an airstrip in Santa Ana, California, which is now one of the runways at John Wayne Airport.

Around the same time, in 1948, Robert E. Petersen, a former publicist from the movie industry, saw the potential in promoting the burgeoning hot rod scene and created *Hot Rod* magazine. Petersen soon realized that he was more of a business and idea man than a magazine editor. He convinced Wally Parks to take on the role of editor of *Hot Rod*, and the two helped to guide the magazine as well as the entire hot rodding world. That relationship, and their desire to bring hot rods into the mainstream (and out from under the controversial cloud), begat the formation of the NHRA.

People have been drag racing each other since, it has been said, "the second guy in town got a car." Unorganized and horribly unsafe street races were being held across the country in the late 1940s, and it got to the point that both law enforcement and the public at large had had just about enough. The term "hot rodder" was a bad thing back then; kind of how "gang banger" is today.

The NHRA's primary mission was to reverse that and, in Wally's words, "create order from chaos." *Hot Rod* magazine was exploding in circulation, and its editor, therefore, had the congregation of hot rodders to preach to about safety, legitimatization, and public service instead of public nuisance.

Danny Ongais and Mickey Thompson

Danny Ongais and I have known each other since I was 16, and I was truly sweet on him. He used to come to Georgia and my mother and whole family loved him. His grandfather named all 23 of his kids out of the bible.

Once I went to his homeland of Hawaii with him, and it was sensational. We lived natively off the land, eating papaya and coconut. Danny could climb a tree like a monkey and grab that coconut, run down, chop the top off, and hand it to me to drink. Then he took the knife and carved out the coconut. My God, I was in Hawaiian heaven!

Danny was a fantastic competitor in both IndyCar and drag racing, but of course he started in drag racing and did some motorcycle racing too. I went riding motorcycles with him through the pineapple fields. What a great part of my life. I really treasure those memories.

And the great Mickey Thompson! He and George Hurst were real close, especially when Joe Hrudka and Mickey were partners in some businesses. Amos Satterlee lasted many, many years as Mickey's chief mechanic and then for a lot of other teams.

And I loved *Old Blue*, that bad-ass Mustang Funny Car. It revolutionized Funny Car design in 1969. There were actually two of them, but they were slightly different. Danny drove one and the car's designer/builder Pat Foster drove the other one. Mickey and his guys basically used Top Fuel Dragsters but put a Funny Car body on them, and they ran really good. Danny won in Dallas and then at "The Big Go," the U.S. Nationals in Indianapolis. And they had real Ford engines in them too (427 SOHC Cammers).

Standing between two legends and great friends: Daniel Ezekiel Ongais and Mickey Thompson, with Amos Satterlee next to Mickey. This was after Mickey's Old Blue *Mustang Funny Car had just won. This was taken during one of the sweetest years of my life.*

This was after a parade lap at the NHRA Winternationals in Pomona, California, my first time at that race. George Hurst backed up the car in front of the main grandstands, and I didn't know if I'd be accepted in California because I wasn't a movie star or anything, but the fans were wonderful. That track in Pomona was the fastest I'd seen and had the most Top Fuel dragsters I'd ever seen at one time.

They all came to qualify for the Winternationals; it was like all the drag races I had ever been to piled into one. It was huge, enormous; and I loved the nitromethane smell. I just loved it and still do today. There's nothing like standing on the starting line at Pomona, with my eyes tearing up and my makeup smearing.

George Hurst and Jack Duffy didn't miss a thing. They parked the car right in front of the grandstands two days in a row, and we watched the races from there.

This was the first photo ever taken of me at an NHRA drag race, the 1966 Winternationals in Pomona, California. The car was the Pontiac Bonneville that George had given me with the big gold Hurst shifter handle. This photo shows the first time that he backed me up to the grandstands in front of all the fans, like we did so many times. I remember being a nervous wreck right here; I didn't know if the fans would like me, and how it was all going to work out. Plus, we were right up against the grandstands and I was supposed to do a bow; you can see in my eyes that I was just hoping I didn't rip my jumpsuit and show them all a Moon pie!

I was scared to death but everybody was just so great to me, always have been. Wally and the NHRA family are a big part of my life still, even though Wally passed away a few years ago. This was my introduction to the world of NHRA drag racing, a world that I still live in and love with all my heart.

Buster Couch was the legendary starter for the NHRA for a long time, and he was quite a character to say the least. He always wore cowboy boots on the starting line, and it was his way or the highway; if a racer didn't know that at first, he would soon after he disobeyed one of Buster's orders. Buster and I developed a routine every time I was at a drag race. I'd stop the Hurst car on the line, bend down, and give him a kiss. It became a ritual that was popular with the fans, and his wife even approved. I think these photos were taken at Sanair in Canada. (Bob McClurg Photos)

The first official NHRA drag race was held in April 1953, at the Los Angeles County Fairgrounds in Pomona, a suburb just east of Los Angeles. I was too young to attend that event; the Winternationals at Pomona in 1966 was the first drag race I ever worked for Hurst. I had been to a drag race before Pomona, mind you; I used to go to a lot of match races and the like with Don Garlits, but I had never been to a national event until I won Miss Hurst Golden Shifter and went to the Winternationals. I had never seen so many good-looking men, and all those dragsters in one place! I think they had 100 Top Fuel dragsters back then. It was crazy. Ever since that 1966 Winternationals, I have never missed an NHRA race at Pomona, and I've also attended every one of the U.S. Nationals at Indianapolis Raceway Park since that year.

"I had never seen so many good-looking men, and all those dragsters in one place!"

"Gentleman Joe" Schubeck

One of my best friends in all of drag racing and definitely someone I consider my brother is "Gentleman Joe" Schubeck. He built one of the first tube-chassis dragsters in the late 1950s and used it to start the Lakewood Chassis Company. Lakewood became famous for its blow-proof bellhousings that contained clutch explosions, greatly increasing safety for both the drivers and spectators.

Joe became part of our Hurst family in 1966 when George asked him to drive a sister car to the Hurst *Hemi Under Glass* that Bob Riggle was piloting, only Schub's car would have two blown, nitro-burning Oldsmobile engines powering slicks on all four wheels and making more than 2,500 hp. The idea behind the Hurst *Hairy Olds* was to smoke all four tires the length of the quarter-mile as an exhibition car to get the crowd going crazy.

Schub was hesitant, but then George showed him a photo and said, "I want you to see the new girl I'm going to hire for Miss Golden Shifter. Her name is Linda Vaughn, and she'll be there to take your top hat and your white gloves and help you get in the car, and she'll be part of the pit crew." Schubeck was sold on the project, and Jim Dietz agreed to make him a fire suit befitting the nickname "Gentlemen Joe." The tuxedo-like suit included long tails and it even had a fireproof bow tie!

Schub was a member of SEMA's Board of Directors and was a pioneer on the safety committee, and we just put him into the SEMA Hall of Fame in 2013. I still see him all the time; we have lunch, see each other at various functions, and he came with me when I was put into the Motorsports Hall of Fame, the second woman honored there, after Shirley Muldowney.

Who else but George Hurst, one of the greatest promoters in the world of drag racing, would introduce

a new exhibition car, following up his already famous *Hemi Under Glass*, with Top Fuel Driver Joe Schubeck' driving the first-time introduction of the Hurst *Hairy Olds* on its debut at the Bakersfield March Meet, in front of every Top Fuel dragster team lined up on the fire-up road ready and waiting for eliminations to start?

Joe Schubeck:

"*Hairy Olds* was sitting on the starting line and I, dressed in a lavish Deist tuxedo fire suit with tails that Liberace would have been proud to wear at his piano, came out of the sky in a helicopter and landed on the starting line with none other than the Lovely Linda Vaughn in the most beautiful black evening dress and looking like she is ready to step onto the stage of the Academy Awards.

"Linda, in all her splendor, helped me get ready to give the March Meet fans a first look at the Hurst *Hairy Olds*. First taking my top hat, white gloves, and cane, she helped me into the seat. After a 'Best wishes,' I was ready to fire up both engines and blast off on the car's maiden voyage. A first!"

Here I am with Mike Sirokan at Bakersfield in 1996.

Bob Riggle and the Hurst Hemi Under Glass *Barracuda. Like the Hurst* Hairy Olds, Hemi Under Glass *was an exhibition car to both promote the Hurst brand and bring excitement to the fans. The Barracuda had a nitromethane-burning Chrysler Hemi under the rear window, so that the rearward weight bias would make it wheel-stand the length of the track. Wild Bill Shrewsberry helped design the car and Bob Riggle, who was a mechanic and fabricator for Hurst, drove it.*

" I first met Linda in 1967 just after the Airheart Disc Brake Company was purchased by Hurst Performance. I had arrived in Sebring and went to a mansion that George Hurst had rented. Jack Duffy met me at the door and I joined them for breakfast. During breakfast one of the most beautiful women I have ever seen was introduced to me and I think I stuck my spoon of cereal in my ear! That was the beginning of us working together for the next 11 years.

"It's very difficult to put in words what an outstanding lady Linda is. We worked open houses, NHRA races, NASCAR, and of course the Indy 500. Linda is uncanny in how she is able to work with anyone; from the person on the street to CEOs of large companies. Her memory of people's names is amazing. Recently I took Linda to a "Geritol Gang" old-timers go-kart drivers reunion and she remembered the names of people she hadn't seen in 40 years!

"Sure, there are many stories I can tell about Linda, but I would have to censor them before telling them. Bottom line is that I am proud to call Linda a longtime friend and neighbor. I've loved her for a long time. "

— Bob Airheart

In the winner's circle with Bob Airheart on the right and a racer trying to talk me into a kiss. I remember thinking, "I don't know about that" and wasn't going for it. Bob is another brother of mine, and when he got inducted into the SEMA Hall of Fame, he thanked me for helping him get there. I was so happy, proud, and impressed that night.

This is Ben Green, who owned Dallas Raceway, and his wife, Sally Green. Ben was a sweet man and always ran a great racetrack, but it was the sight of some tragedy. Pat Foster (in Mickey Thompson's other Mustang Funny Car) and Gerry Schwartz had a mid-track collision at the 1969 NHRA Springnationals there, and Gerry was killed. I do remember that when this photo was taken, Raymond Beadle's Blue Max won the race.

Dickey Harrell in the winner's circle again, with the Mr. Gibbs Chevrolet. That's Nikki Phillips on the far right.

Dyno Don Nicholson in Texas when he won Super Stock. Dyno lived right down the road from me in Georgia, and when I moved to California he also moved to California. He was such a sweet man. I did the invocation at the NHRA Museum funeral service.

In the winner's circle (from left): Don Garlits, Dickey Harrell, me, and AHRA President Jim Tice. Garlits won Top Fuel and Dickey Harrell won Funny Car in the Mr. Gibb Chevrolet Camaro at this race.

Dickey Harrell was so precious and I loved him so much! I've never been a drinker, but as you can see here, we didn't have any champagne glasses so I took a swig right from the bottle.

His daughter still stays in touch with me. Did you know he died to save others? When that left front tire blew in Toronto and he got killed, I was there. All these years later, he's still a hero in all of our eyes. I even had a little crush on him.

Big Daddy Don Garlits, after he won a race. My mother made that gold lamé suit for me and I also had a little jacket. Like most of my outfits, I still have it somewhere, up in my attic. One day I'll find them all.

Below: Another shot of Mike Sirokan of The Surfers, at Bakersfield in 1966. I wonder what that guy in the background is thinking. Probably, "How am I going to get that trophy on the trailer?" Mike was a real fine young man, a real sweetheart, and was the first Southern California drag racer that I got to know. He was sponsored by Engle Cams, and I knew all of them.

This was the first time I went to Bakersfield and I didn't know if anyone was going to like me or not. But I guess they did, and everyone was real sweet to me. All of those California drivers fascinate me. I'd read about them in the magazines for years so it was fun to finally meet them all.

Mike got in that car in Bakersfield and had a real heavy foot, and won that race over about 100 other Top Fuel cars. That event was also memorable because they had the Hell's Angels directing traffic.

Pat Garlits with her and Don's daughters Gaylynn and Donna. What a wonderful family; I grew up with the Garlits family. Pat just passed away not long before we started working on this book, and I miss her. Don was devastated when she passed. She was always by his side, and I still stay in touch with him and the girls. I never had children because everyone else's kids were my kids.

At the same 1966 Bakersfield Smokers Meet with Goober Tuller and Freight Train. *He was a tiny guy but he got a good smooch from me, as you can see.*

This was taken at Orange County International Raceway in Southern California, 1974. That's me with Miss Orange County Raceway. (Howard Coby Photo)

This was at an IHRA race at Bristol, which we did as well as NHRA and AHRA races. Anywhere there was a drag race, Hurst and I were there! (Photo Courtesy Bristol Dragway)

Platte and Payne

The famous Platte and Payne at Georgia Dragstrip. I was lying on the car and we were all BS'ing with each other. Hubert was probably saying to me, "Do you have any more of your daddy's moonshine?" They always had white lightning with them and I didn't like it, but I'd take it and tell them I was going to rub it on my mosquito bites!

They were running at Yellow River the next day, and at 4:00 in the morning they came banging on my door, woke me up, and said, "Hey, you got any whiskey Linda? We gotta finish the car. We worked all night and we're thirsty."

I said, "Well see what's in there." It was a bottle of Jack Daniels so I told them to go ahead and take it. They took it, finished the car, and got out there the next afternoon and won that damn race! Can you believe that? Hubert Platt and Randy Payne. They're Georgia boys so they're some of my brothers.

We just lost Hubert and his wife Linda called me upon his passing and I thanked her for sharing all the good years we've had together.

Randy Payne:

"Being a part of the Ford Drag Team has allowed me to meet many wonderful people and I am thankful to have had that opportunity. Linda will always hold a part of my heart. We are dear friends.

"To Hubert and all my racing friends, we will stage it up again someday.

"I would also like to thank Ford Motor Company for giving me this unique opportunity. Remember, you can't put a price on a good time."

"Drag racing gets in your blood, just like NASCAR and IndyCar. It's my addiction. I don't drink; I go racing."

Drag racing gets in your blood, just like NASCAR and IndyCar. It's my addiction. I don't drink; I go racing. One time, a lady reporter from New York City came to the U.S. Nationals in Indianapolis to do a story on racing, with the mindset that drugs were a big part. I took her down to the starting line at the U.S. Nationals and said, "Now, breathe *this!*"

She turned to me and screamed, "Oh Lawd, this is louder than Ted Nugent!"

Her eyes were burning, her nose was burning, everything was on fire from the nitromethane, and I said, "Now *that's* our drug!" There's nothing like nitromethane, but I also love the Pro Stock and Gas classes. I love it all.

I really enjoyed promoting drag racing. I had already become established in NASCAR and IndyCar as Miss Firebird, so when I was at one of those races I also made sure that I could promote the drag racing world. When I'd go to

Back in Pomona at the Winternationals in 1974, when one of my heroes, Bill "Grumpy" Jenkins won Pro Stock. The girl on the left was one of my Hurstettes and was a graduate of Pepperdine University.

This was a race at Orange County International Raceway in 1974, after Don Garlits won Top Fuel.

This is with Don "The Snake" Prudhomme and engine builder Ed Pink at the SEMA Hall of Fame luncheon. Pink was being so serious and Snake said something funny or stupid, and I was cracking up. Pink was Cool Hand Luke here; he's not even cracking a smile. I'm not going to tell you what they were saying because it's not family friendly, but it was funny! Snake and Ed have been great friends of mine since the beginning of this whole ride.

Dave Strickler drove Grumpy's Toy, and this is him talking to Nikki and me. Nikki is so sweet and brilliant; she was always pulling stuff out of the woods and sticking it in a jar. She was really into all kinds of plants.

With Raymond Beadle's **Blue Max** *in Texas. That's Junebug on the right and Miss Springnationals on the left (she may have been Miss Texas at the time as well). Raymond Beadle was another brother of mine, and he was in a class of his own. The first time I met Raymond was a long, long time ago, in Dalton, Georgia, when they had a poker game with Buster Couch and my folks, a bunch of people.*

When my brother told me later that Raymond Beadle was going to drive the Blue Max *Funny Car, I went to the drag races, walked over to talk to him and said, "Remember when you was playing poker with my daddy and Buster?" We instantly became friends.*

My whole family knows Mongoose McEwen, Snake Prudhomme, Raymond Beadle, and Richard Tharp; they're all brothers. Beadle was a good-old slow-talkin' cowboy from down in Texas, but when he got in that car he hauled ass. He was a great friend.

Ronnie Sox, of the Sox & Martin Pro Stock team at Bristol. He always used to say "beautiful, just beautiful." Ronnie's another brother of mine. He and I were great buddies.

Daytona for the 500, I would be on radio and television shows talking about racing and of course Hurst, but I would also try to promote drag racing whenever I had the opportunity.

One time a sports writer told me, "Drag racing is a dirty, grease-under-your-fingernails sport."

I answered, "No it isn't; you race on Sunday and sell on Monday in drag racing just like you do in NASCAR, maybe even more. There are test pilots out there for cars and parts. You need to go see a drag race, mister, and you'll see what I mean." He finally did, and I won't tell you who that guy was, but he sure wrote some good articles on drag racing.

In the course of writing this book, I was asked about my favorite moments in drag racing, and it's very hard to put a finger on. Just like it's impossible for a mother to say which is her favorite child, I can't really do that about any of my racing experiences. When it comes to just drag racing though, I have to say that it is when Tom "The Mongoose" McEwen won the U.S. Nationals right after losing his son, in 1978. He raced Don "The Snake" Prudhomme in the finals and beat Snake. We all rushed down to the finish line and I was one of the first people to greet Tom, and we cried so hard. That was a very heartfelt day.

There were also times with Snake, Bill "Grumpy" Jenkins, Don Garlits, Sox & Martin, Dick Landy . . . it was so exciting every year, every race. Picking favorite moments in drag racing is like making a chocolate cake and putting frosting on top. "How much do you want? How much you got?" Racing is my addiction, and it's impossible to choose one when I've had many a favorite time.

Roy Hill

❚❚I had an involvement with the Pettys so I knew of Linda Vaughn when she was doing the NASCAR races as Miss Firebird, and the respect the Pettys had for her spread to me. I first met her in the early 1970s; I had been around her some in the 1960s and she remembered my association with the Pettys, and she remembered my name! The Pettys built me a '72 Duster drag car, and I can remember they told Linda to look after me when I came drag racing, and she did.

She's the first lady of racing period. I guess it was in Indianapolis, at the *Car Craft* All Star Team banquet; she took me by the hand and took me around meeting people and sat me down at her table. That started a wonderful relationship that people can only dream about. I went racing, I did pretty well, and she was as proud of me as I guess anyone could be.

"I've seen so many lives affected by her. She affected my life, my career, my personal life so much. I met her mother, went to the house, knew her sisters; she was just roughly 400 miles from me in Georgia so I'd go down and spend time with them; we'd go water skiing or just have fun. I was always there for her, to pick her up at the airport and things; whatever she needed me to do, whenever she asked me to do it.

"There's just so much that she did for me, for my career. As time went on with Chrysler, running the Petty Duster and the Plymouth Arrows and the Dodge Colts, the Horizons, things like that, then I switched to Fords. And I'll never forget this: We were in Columbus, Ohio, for the Summernationals and the *Chi-Town Hustler* had oiled the track down and it took about two hours to clean it up. When people oiled the track down, they'd

Roy Boy at Gainesville. Do you drink white lightning? Because Roy sure does! I met Roy in the early 1960s over some moonshine. My daddy made peach brandy. Roy was going to drive for Richard Petty in a drag race car, but his hair was too long and he was a mess. I said, "Roy, we're going to have to cut your hair, clean up your mess, and help you." So we did and he started driving drag cars for Petty.

Maurice Petty is one of Roy's best friends. I'd go by to see them and we'd hang out. Roy came to my house in Georgia and I asked him if he knew how to waterski. He said, "Hell no." So I told him we were going to teach him. We took him to the lake, I taught him how to waterski, and we just became bonded, spent so much time together.

There's something about waterskiing and lakes, I swear. I went over to the Petty party at Maurice and Richard's. Roy was driving Hillbilly and Hurst and Richard were sponsoring it (we made his shifters).

Roy was a hell of a Pro Stock driver, and then he had the idea for the driving school and Hurst sponsored that too. We've always been business friends, and done some shows together. I never could drink that white lightning though. I could run it in the race cars but there ain't no damn way I'm gonna drink it!

Roy became part of the family and he'd stop in and see Mother a lot. We are a close-knit group, and Roy and Booper were real good friends. I call him Roy Boy my Love Joy. He says "L. V., I luuuuv yoo." I've known all his wives too!

Roy Hill *CONTINUED*

do interviews with drivers and different things in the tower. I had sold my Horizon right there at the track so I was in the tower on the PA system talking.

" I got a chance to talk for more than two hours about not just the drivers, but also the crew chiefs, the crew members, and their sponsors. I remember coming down out of the tower and Linda hugged my neck and said, 'You said things that we've all wanted to say for years and didn't know how to say.'

"She introduced me to Gene Dicolla, the head of Ford Motorcraft. I had built a Ford Mustang and Jack Roush was doing the engines. I was going to Detroit the following week to pick up some engines and Gene told me to come by his office and talk when I came to Detroit. This is when Raymond Beadle, Billy Meyer, and Bob Glidden had the Ford deal, and Kenny Bernstein had the Lincoln Mercury deal. I heard that the head of Lincoln Mercury's motorsports program was there, and I got to meet him too.

"Then Linda and I went into the pits at a race and she introduced me to Ernie Beckman, who later was over all of Ford Racing for a few years. That started the relationship with Lincoln Mercury (with the Capri) in 1983, and later on I switched over to Ford, and I'm still with them now. Linda Vaughn was the reason that it all got started.

"She introduced me to Roger Penske, to so many people. She always made me feel like I was something, like I was a million dollars, and I've always had the respect for her and showed that back to her in any way I could. She is a business lady, a beautiful lady, and a great person to represent any company that she is involved with.

"A few years ago we went to her roast in Indianapolis at Forrest

Lucas's mansion, and I was so proud of all the people that came and what they had to say about her. There are so, so many people whose careers have gone somewhere because of Linda Vaughn. I can't say enough for what she's done for me. My wife loves her, we all love her, and not just here in the South, but all over the world."

I love this picture! Two of my most lovable loves right here: Roy Hill (left) and Paul Candies, sitting on the guardrail before the start of pro runs, talking about business and getting Roy another car.

I told them "I love you two" and was holding Paul's hand. I think Roy was jealous. Anything I could do to help them I would.

Paul Candies was very much "in the know" with the business world. He was sponsored by Schiefer Clutches and was in the background in the business; he kept me informed on the big end of the business, like when Hurst went public. He knew things I didn't know, and we had a phone call at least once a week. I really miss him.

And Roy? I went to his drag racing school and he kept me after class. But I took him an apple!

66 Winning a Top Fuel race and having my lifelong friend Linda Vaughn in the winner's circle with me was a childhood dream come true. I first met her in the early 1970s. Even though I was only a teenager we instantly clicked and we have been best friends ever since.

"I have been fortunate to have countless Linda Vaughn moments in the Winner's Circle, and if for some reason she wasn't there, it didn't feel the same. She is a brick in the foundation of our sport. 99

— Darrell Gwynn

This is Darrell Gwynn and his daddy Jerry, in Seattle, at his last win. Right after this he went to England and crashed, which paralyzed him. That's when he started his Darrell Gwynn Foundation to help people with spinal cord injuries. Darrell was my date for the Motorsports Hall of Fame induction at the Waldorf Astoria in New York City when they inducted Chip Ganassi into the Hall. I was very proud to be there with both of them.

This is Victory Circle at Ontario (California) with Jim Dunn, me, Grumpy, and Tami Pittman, and Don Moody. Tami was one of my Hurstettes and was K. S. Pittman's daughter. Based on our reactions, Dunn was telling one of his usual off-the-wall, fire-burning stories! We had such a ritual in Victory Circle; it was so much fun. I could always make Grumpy smile. And you can see that Mother cut my outfit a little short here. You can see my underpants!

Bill "Grumpy" Jenkins is one of my true heroes, along with Junior Johnson, Richard Petty, Mario Andretti, A. J. Foyt, and others.

Grumpy, up to no good! He had his hand on my shoulder, squeezing it, and I'm cracking up. We were talking about some situation or another. Grumpy and I were inseparable.

This is the last picture I took of Grumpy. He died in 2012, and I really miss him.

My mother just loved Big Daddy, and she always had a smile on her face when he was around. He and I have been friends for a long time, starting when I was about 14 years old in Dalton, Georgia. This photo was taken at the NHRA Hot Rod Reunion in Bakersfield. Mother, of course, had to go over and get a hug from Big Daddy.

Me and Jeg Coughlin Sr., of Jeg's Speed Shop and mail order chain. I went to all of their weddings. I knew Daddy and his daddy when he ran Top Fuel dragsters. I used to do all the Jeg's store openings and we sold a lot of Hurst shifters through Jeg's. The Coughlins are my babies, they're part of my family. I call them family.

This was after the races and my Jeg's boys won in both Pro Stock Truck and Pro Stock. That's daddy Jeg, Jessie "Little Bitter" Colter, and me. She even drove a Top Fuel dragster once.

From left to right are Shirley Muldowney, me, Donnie Couch, and a fan. This was a special day: Shirley's last run at Pomona, on the last day. I drug out my pink outfits and she wore the pink jacket I'd given her. Donnie Couch worked on the car; he has worked with everybody.

This is Booper and me with Shirley at Irwindale, at the Hangover Nationals in 1971 or 1972 on New Year's Day. Booper and I weren't even working. We just drove out there to see everyone. I had to drive because Booper was huuuuuung over. I'm pretty sure Shirley won the race!

Shirley and Barbara Parks (when Shirley won the Winternationals) with her dog Skippy. Skippy loved me. That dog would sit in the seat until Shirley got ready to do her burnout and when she did the burnout Skippy would run under the seat. As soon as she popped the 'chute she'd come back up in the seat, and when she got stopped, Skippy would jump up on the tire. Every time. This is a great shot of the leaders of the industry.

This was at the NHRA World Finals at Pomona in 2014, with Shirley in the Legends tent.

This is GaGa, the matriarch of the Coughlin family, the mother of Jeg Coughlin Sr. and grandmother to Jeg Jr., Mike, John, and Troy. She was 92 the last time I saw her and just as spry as a Georgia pine. We'd be at the races and she would point at the kids and say, "See, see what I did?"

I told her, "You must have had fun in the backseat of that Chevrolet!" I just love GaGa. (Photo Courtesy Jegs Collection)

This is John Hogan, Larry Schumacher, and a Don Schumacher employee. They're Chicago friends. Hogan used to take care of Tony Schumacher when he was little, and he was Don's chief mechanic when he won the championship. Then he went and helped "Little Schu," who just took the number-one qualifying spot; it was a real fun evening.

Hubert Platt at the Moonshine Festival in Georgia, where they have a lot of old moonshine cars. And of course some white lightnin'!

This was for a Roach T-shirt, with me sitting on Barry Setzer's car. Boy do I wish I had that figure now!

Buddy Martin and Ronnie Sox at Bristol. "Beautiful, just beautiful!"

I did a promotion for Castrol Oil at Maple Grove Raceway in Redding, Pennsylvania. They sponsored the race and I got to stand on the starting line between two dragsters, and I tell you what, everything was standing out after that! That was the strongest force I ever felt in my life. It was fabulous!

At a car show in Miami with Jerry Gwynn's Funny Car. I worked at a lot of car shows, I can tell you that. I'm sure this was used in one of my Hurst ads. What a great family, the Gwynns.

With "Akron Arlen" Vanke in 1966. Do you think I had enough hair?

Courtney Force and I. But this isn't at a drag race; it's at the Indianapolis 500 in 2014. I was standing in Dario Franchitti's pit when she came walking by and we took the photo. I couldn't figure out why she was there, but then I watched her walk over to Graham Rahal's pit and I figured it out. They were just recently married.

“ As a kid growing up out on the NHRA circuit watching my dad race, I remember the first time I met Linda Vaughn. She was beautiful, bubbly, and so kind. My dad explained to me how well known she was as Miss Hurst and I remember being in awe and asking him so many questions. I thought it was so cool that a woman was so into cars, knowledgable, and loved by so many, in all levels of motorsports. She squeezed me tight and gave me a red smooch on my cheek. She was so friendly and acted as if we'd known each other for years.

"A few years later, I got the opportunity to see and work with Linda at numerous races, car shows, and Mac Tools fairs while I was getting a start in my Funny Car career. We got to know each other best while doing autograph signings at my dad's John Force Racing Holiday Car Show, every December. She was always so encouraging and supportive of what I was trying to accomplish in racing.

"She greeted all fans with a smile and was effortlessly personable with each one making conversation, posing for pictures, and not caring about the two hours plus of signing for the long line of car lovers. Her passion, her strength, her kindness to strangers, and her love of cars and racing has always been admirable being a female in a male-dominated sport and industry.

"She is a role model to many and I'm proud to call Linda my friend. ”

— Courtney Force

This was at Thunder Valley, Bristol. What a great and loud track that was, and with fun, rowdy fans! I loved going to Bristol. Riding in the backseat was Miss Bristol. (Tommy Erwin Photo)

This was one of the times I took my stepsister Sheila Ann to the drag races with me. This is Bristol, and that's "Kansas John" Wiebe's dragster trailer in the background. Wiebe was a three-time AHRA Top Fuel world champion and an NHRA national event winner before he retired in 1977. (Tommy Erwin Photo)

Here I am at Atco Raceway in New Jersey with Miss U.S. Open Drags and our Hurst Olds pace car. I loved that car! (Tommy Erwin Photo)

At the Winternationals in Pomona in either 1968 or 1969, with our Pontiac GTO and the big gold Hurst shifter. Mother, of course, made this outfit and cut out my "peekaboo," as she called it. (James Handy Photo)

Jack Watson, "The Shifty Doc," driving me down the track at Pomona in 1968. Compare that little tower to what they have now at Pomona. I love Pomona and never miss a drag race there. (James Handy Photo)

At Lions Drag Strip, which was managed by the late, great Mickey Thompson. I'm riding the Hurst shifter platform with Jack Jones, the Top Gas racer that was the "model" for the NHRA's famous and highly cherished "Wally" trophy that is given to national event winners. Jack was the model for the bronze trophy, but it was named after NHRA founder Wally Parks, of course.

We did a lot of promotions at the races, handing out prizes and certificates for Hurst and Schiefer Clutches. These guys were both winners at a drag race in Columbus, I think.

My mother loved going to the U.S. Nationals, especially when I'd take her down to the starting line. That's cousin Billie and Booper behind us; we were quite the sight down there! My mother loved Kenny Bernstein and would always say to him, "Hey Bernstein, can't you run a little quicker?"

Dragway 42 outside Chicago! What a place. I heard they're redoing the whole place. Dragway 42 used to have shows with 64 Funny Cars and it was quite a sight! This was with Clare Sanders, his crew, and the trophy with their Ramchargers Funny Car after a win. (Charles Gilchrist Photo)

Shirley Muldowney

A lot of people didn't get along with Shirley, but I did. I was with her through her hard years, getting started, the trips she had to take with the men in the pits. It was brand new and therefore a learning experience for all of us, and she was abused a lot along the way, but she became a national monument for all of us women in the sport. Every time I could help I was there for her, and she was there for me.

One day I saw a bunch of mothers standing there with their daughters and she was shaking all over, angry about the car and everything. I said, "Shirley, lower your voice and smile at those kids," and I went and took care of it for her. I walked over and explained that, "Shir-

ley's upset right now because they have to change the engine."

And I went back to Shirley and said, "You have to quit talking like that because it's hurting you. You don't realize who that might be. That may very well be a potential sponsor with their little girls, and you have to curtail your mouth. I'll be your mouth for you, I'll do anything for you because we're going to win this championship."

I stuck to her like glue that year. We won Columbus and in Victory Circle I said, "Hell, I ain't never kissed a woman in Victory Circle before!" And I kissed her on the cheek.

Shirley Muldowney CONTINUED

I became real close friends with her; she looked after me and I looked after her and we were a good team, and we worked on a lot of promotions over the years. We still are good friends. She was called "Cha Cha" early in her career, but I stopped calling her that early on. Although I always told her, like George Hurst had told me, "As long as they spell your name right, publicity's publicity."

I think she's had a hard life, a tough life, but I admire her stamina and qualities. I saw some of the nastiness, but I was there for her. Her sister's name is Linda and her mother's name is Mae and my mother's name is Mae. She's also a great cook, and she damn sure can drive the heck out of a race car.

Shirley Muldowney:

"This photo was during a national event, I think it was Columbus, and Linda would stop by periodically during the weekend and we'd share, you know, girl talk. She was pretty personable and up on just about everything that was going on. I knew I was always in store for a good story when Linda arrived!

"Linda was and still is a goodwill ambassador, very popular in the sport and a very pretty lady, and she has had a lot of longevity in the sport. I can't say we were bosom buddies and hung out, since I was pretty busy and didn't have any, that I can think of, really close friends in the sport that took my time away from my job. That was to drive the race car, run the race car, be nursemaid, financier, referee. Just about everything that goes along with a four-man crew and keeping your head above water in the sport.

"Back then it was such a money pit, and today it's a money *quarry*! They've made the sport almost impossible for any young hopeful or aspiring driver to get the chance other than being at the right place at the right time, or having a daddy with deep pockets."

Don "The Snake" Prudhomme

Between my boys, Mongoose (left) and Snake, at the Winternationals in 2014; we were in the Legends Parade together at that event. Snake is such a sweetheart and Goose bitched the whole way down the track, but I love 'em both! About Don Prudhomme, my mother always used to say, "You know, snakes crawl at night." (Tom Siekfer Photo)

❚❚ I was just a young kid coming up and I knew Linda as Miss Hurst Golden Shifter, but I didn't really know anything about NASCAR or the things she'd done before that. Coming from the South, she was heavy in the NASCAR scene, so when she came over into drag racing as Miss Hurst, we were in awe of her because she was like Marilyn Monroe, larger than life, and obviously she was gorgeous. And up until that time, it was fairly risqué, with the big boobs and her body and her hair. All the guys loved it of course. She brought the sex, the class, all of that into drag racing.

"Before that, we were a bunch of greasy T-shirt guys, and to see someone like that come into the sport, I thought to myself, 'Man I'd better dress a little nicer. Maybe I can get a kiss on the cheek from her.' I had to clean up my act, and I think we all did trying to impress her.

"The thing about her, you become real close to her. She never forgets anybody's name and for some reason we really hit it off well. I got to know her mom and she was like family after a while. Obviously, she still had this great body and a bigger-than-life attitude but she was like family, and still is.

"It's amazing how she is still marching on. I'll turn around at some show and there's Linda. Or I'll turn on the TV and there's Linda. I don't know how the hell she gets around so much.

"Of course we had a lot of fun together. I remember a time when James Garner, Linda, and I were at the Speedway. I was walking down the hallway in the hotel and the door was open to Garner's room and they were in there partying, so I just went in and joined them. I thought that was the coolest. Can you imagine a young buck like me and all of a sudden here's Linda and Garner and we're all sitting there hanging out, and I thought 'Wow, Linda's really cool.' She's just the coolest chick ever.

"It's odd how this sex symbol becomes your sister in a way. I think we have this certain bond with one another and I treasure it. She's always telling me 'snakes crawl at night' in that Southern accent. She's a good ol' Southern gal, man; it don't come much better than that."

This is at the **Hot Rod** *magazine drags at Riverside (California) and that's Tom "Mongoose" McEwen, probably trying to proposition me as you can tell by the intense conversation we were having. We were actually in a deep conversation right there, I think because he had to run Muldowney. And she was tough to beat. Tom and I have been and always will be great friends.*

" The first time I met Linda was in 1966 at the *Hot Rod* Magazine Nationals at Riverside Raceway in California. We won that race and she was Miss Hurst Golden Shifter and the queen of the race. I've known her ever since then, in drag racing and over all the years.

"We're good friends and she's an excellent people person, always talking to people, and she's always nice and remembers everyone's name. Everybody around the racing world just loves her. She's a beautiful lady with great experiences and is personable and kind to everyone. She was always a great ambassador for the sport and I enjoy her friendship still today. "

— Tom McEwen

I absolutely love this photo! This is McEwen, June Cochran, John Hogan (the chief mechanic in the Snake and Mongoose Revel days) and I at the U.S. Nationals in Indianapolis.

This is at the drag races at Sanair in 1978. My brown leather vest was made by an artist near where I live in Laguna Beach, California, and I paired it with a Shady Brady hat, a pair of Mother's cut-off jeans, and that dark California suntan. Hot stuff there! (Photo Courtesy Bob Boudreau)

This was at Bakersfield. We made these cutouts early in the Hurst days, and this man had two of them. One was faded after being in his store window for 30 years, and he had a second one he bought on eBay for $500. Mother sweet-talked him out of the faded one, and I still have it in my home office.

Bob McClurg

All photos are courtesy of Bob McClurg.

"Linda Vaughn and I definitely have some 'history' together. Like most young guys, she was my pin-up queen in the early days before I was able to break into the drag racing photography game. That all changed at the 1968 U.S. Nationals at Indy, when Fram Corporation hired me to photograph the event for them. I was able to meet and get to know L. V. through the Fram guys. I was in hog heaven when she and I posed for a picture taken by the late Les Lovett.

"As the years passed, Linda and I continued our friendship and she was one of my greatest supporters. Through the years Linda and I have gone through a lot. As acting public relations man for the N. T. Yowell Movers Pro Stock Racing Team (Dayton, Ohio) I was the one responsible for getting boss Neil Yowell, a successful United Van Lines Moving Company franchisee, to move Linda from Atlanta to California. One of the guys from Yowell Movers and I drove down to Atlanta and I photographed/publicized the packing process.

"I got to know Linda's mother Mae (whom I adored)

and sister Sheila real well. In fact, I dated Sheila a couple of times and still stay in contact with her. To this day, L. V. is still trying to get the two of us to hook up. Linda also repeatedly tried to get me a job with Hurst Performance, but the timing never seemed right.

"Probably the biggest charge I get out of knowing Linda Vaughn is that even to this day, whenever we're at a car show and she's there signing autographs, she'll stop what she's doing to talk to me. She always calls me 'Lil Brother' or 'Bobby.' You should see the looks I get from guys standing in line. It's like, 'Who the hell is this guy?' And it feels really great!"

Linda Vaughn:

"Bob was such a sweetheart, and we struck up a friendship right off the bat.

"Bob always had a habit of not remembering girls' names, so he'd just squeeze them a little tighter!

"When I got the 'brownlines' for my *Here's Linda Vaughn* book, Bob took a picture of me reading them. People paid $1 for this book in 1971 and really good copies of them sell for well over $100 on eBay today."

Bob McClurg *CONTINUED*

"This was at the U.S. Nationals in Indy, 1968, the first time I ever met L. V. I was working there for FRAM Corporation as a photographer and Les Lovett took this picture using my Mamiya 2-1/4 camera. I was in hog heaven!"

"This photo was taken by either Jim Kelly or Jeff Tinsley at the AHRA Winter Nationals in Phoenix circa 1971, using my Hasselblad camera. By then L. V. and I were becoming good friends. Dig that crazy mustache; on me, not Linda!"

"I shot this photo of L. V. at the same Phoenix AHRA race, while she was reading her new book Here's Linda Vaughn. Those books now sell on eBay for upwards of $100."

"The NHRA Springnationals at Dallas International Motor Speedway in 1969 while I was working for Super Stock & Drag Illustrated as their photo editor. I believe Jim McCraw took this photo using my Hasselblad camera. In this photo I'm sandwiched between Linda and Miss NHRA Springnationals but I'm sorry, I can't remember her name. Nice place to be, eh?"

" Here are Linda and me in the staging lanes at what looks to be Pomona with the Pro Stock truck. Linda was a big fan of the trucks because they were, of course, stick shifts! She even took the time to find some material-covered Hurst T-handles for me! "

— Mike Coughlin

Mike Coughlin when he won in his Pro Stock Truck at Pomona. Little did we know that Pro Stock Truck was going to be wiped out right after this. I was proud of the Pro Stock Trucks and I was so disappointed when the NHRA pulled the trucks out. I thought it was a silly political bureaucratic move, and I raised hell because I had represented them. I did everything I could to keep it going because people loved them, and when you went out in any parking lot, most of the vehicles were trucks. So it didn't make a lot of sense to me.

My boss these days is Chevrolet Performance, who I represent at a lot of events. These were taken at the NHRA World Finals at Pomona in 2014. The Chevrolet Performance trailer is on the Manufacturer's Midway at the races, and I sign autographs and take pictures with fans. I love talking to the fans, from those who knew me in the 1960s to the young kids just learning about drag racing.

In the tower at Pomona with Ed "The Ace" McCullough, one of the finest Funny Car drivers ever. That's John Lombardo standing behind him. Ed was very fond of my Hurstettes. I always called him brother. He's a fine, fine man, a true gentleman of the sport. Just stay away from K. S. Pittman's daughter, Ed!

If Pro Stock is running, I'm on the mic in the announcer's booth. I love my Pro Stock boys and girls, and announcing during their runs is one of the great joys of my life. Here I am announcing Pro Stock with Alan Reinhardt.

"Picking favorite moments in drag racing is like making a chocolate cake and putting frosting on top. "How much do you want? How much you got?"

One of the highest, most coveted awards that the NHRA has is the Public Relations Award, and they gave it to little ol' me in 1970. This is NHRA founder Wally Parks presenting it to me. I loved Uncle Wally and I have that plaque hanging in my hallway at home. It's an honor that I was very, very proud of, one of my first such honors, and I was absolutely thrilled to death that night!

Presenting the 1971 Public Relations Award to the Sox & Martin Racing team. What great men I've gotten to work with, and I'm incredibly honored to call them my dear friends.

5 NASCAR

There are three races that I never miss: The NHRA U.S. Nationals in Indianapolis, the Indianapolis 500, and the Daytona 500. Of the three, my first love is NASCAR and especially Daytona; stock car racing in general really, because it was my first exposure to the Big Time. My first trip to Daytona was when I was Miss Atlanta Raceway in 1961.

Organizing Bootleggers

Back then, the big NASCAR races had a parade for all the pace cars from the tracks on the racing schedule. The lead pace car at a race was the one from the track that was next on the schedule. Because Atlanta was the next race on the schedule, our pace car was in the front of the pack. Jack and Glenda Black and I drove our Pontiac pace car down to Daytona, and that was my first time seeing the track. I had listened to the Daytona 500 on the radio for years but I had never been there, and that first trip in 1961 was the start of a love affair. Daytona and Indianapolis are two of the most intriguing racetracks in the entire world. I'd put them against any track in the world, and I've been all over the world. Daytona is its own lady, its own entity.

Mr. Bill France Sr. was always so kind to us, and he's always been one of my biggest heroes. Think about what he did: He got all of those bootleggers that were racing the 'shine runners and corralled them into an organized racing body with actual rules. Whenever two men each have a car, you just know they're going to race each other. That's just the competitive spirit that exists in almost everyone, but those bootleggers were especially competitive. They raced all over the place, including on the beach in Daytona, but there was no real organization to any of it in the early days.

Dale Earnhardt and I at Riverside International Raceway for an IROC race in the mid-1980s. I'm sure he was giving me a little static right here, about my custom-made cowboy hat. He wanted one of those damn hats so bad so I had one for him in a box in the car and gave it to him after that race.

Atlanta Motor Speedway in 1961, in the winner's circle with the handsome Fred Lorenzen. As Miss Atlanta Raceway, I wore an evening dress for the opening ceremonies but changed to my bathing suit (that was sponsored by Catalina) for the winner's circle. (Photo Courtesy Atlanta Motor Speedway)

George Hurst talking to Ozzy Olson, the sponsor for David Pearson and Dan Gurney, at Daytona in 1966. Ozzy made steering wheels and was a multi-billionaire.

This is with Pete Hamilton, I believe, at a circle track trade show. He won in one of the Plymouth Superbird "Wing Cars" that year. Pete was a sweet young man, but we were never real close.

Cale Yarborough won a lot of races over the years. This was one of them, the Daytona 500 in 1968. He won a lot of races that year, I think six of them, and went on to win the Daytona 500 four times. He even raced in the Indianapolis 500 a time or two.

Pennsylvania's own and a dear friend of mine, the great Lincoln Speedway promoter Hilly Rife, with Tommy Moscone and Elmo Langley. We had so much fun with that Holman-Moody Ford. They invited me, and I had never been to Yankeeland before, but Hilly Rife said, "'We'll take good care of you." Tommy runs the track in Atlanta so I knew him.

They did this promotion and they had Richard Petty and I on the radio doing interviews, and they wanted me to dress up so I wore my first mink stole I ever bought and my little crown. I was queen of that Lincoln Speedway in Pennsylvania. I think Richard won the race. It was a dirt track and they completely packed the place. I'm out there in high heel shoes and a mink jacket and I thought I was hot stuff!

"By the time the meeting was over, they had a rough set of rules and a schedule, and NASCAR was born."

Mr. France moved from Washington, D.C., to Daytona Beach during the Great Depression and actually entered the Daytona race in the 1930s, eventually managing the course and promoting a few races before the War, while also running a local service station. He realized that people would enjoy watching these men race each other in their modified cars but it needed a formal organization if it was going to have a future. There was no shortage of racers and spectators in those early days, but the lack of organization meant that every track had a different set of rules; the "tracks" themselves were, in some cases, either horse-racing tracks or makeshift ovals created to bring races to county fairs.

In December 1947, Mr. France held a meeting at the Streamline Hotel in Daytona Beach, inviting those within the racing community with the purpose of organizing them. By the time the meeting was over, they had a rough set of rules and a schedule, and NASCAR was born. When that meeting adjourned, nobody in attendance could have imagined what the new organization would become.

That's John Marcum, the president of the Automobile Racing Club of America (ARCA), kissing me at Daytona, and that's Booper with me. This was when hairnet scarves were popular.

This is my big brother Tiny Lund talking to his little sister. I was worried about his car that day at Atlanta so we were talking about that. Tiny saved Marvin Panch's life at Daytona in 1963. Marvin was testing in a sports car and crashed, then it burst into flames. It was Tiny who pulled him out of the car and saved him. He was my biggest brother, and Mother used to go to his fish camp all the time.

Three of my pals right here, and heroes in the NASCAR world. From left to right are Fred Lorenzen, Bobby Johns, and Fireball Roberts. I just love this picture.

Below: With Richard Petty's car at the Atlanta 500. This was before they built the permanent garages. They used those military-looking tents as the garages back then.

Fred Lorenzen was so handsome. Now you know why I kissed a Yankee!

This was my first year as Miss Hurst Golden Shifter, 1966, presenting Richard Petty with a check from Hurst for his win at a race. In the red outfit is Winkie Louise who took over as Miss Firebird when I became Miss Hurst Golden Shifter, and that's Hurst's Dick Chrysler in the yellow jacket. (Photo Courtesy Smyle Media)

This was at Hilly Rife's Speedway in Pennsylvania, the first Yankee race I ever went to. That's Hilly to the right of me and Jimmy Moffett from Georgia in the hat on the far right. Hilly crowned me the Queen of Speed at this race. He was a great promoter and all the NASCAR boys came and ran his race. Petty, Yarborough, everybody. Richard Petty won the race this night and I was so excited to give Richard a kiss. He had the prettiest teeth! A handsome man, that Richard.

Dale Earnhardt

Dale chased the hell out of me. His daddy was kind of a hero to my mother and we watched Dale get started. I did some work for Wrangler jeans, his major sponsor at the time, and had all my girls in Wranglers. His public relations guy, Joe Whitlock, was putting together this Wrangler promotion so we were all there at Riverside.

We'd go out to dinner and hang out together a lot. I was going through my divorce at the time and Dale wasn't married. He bought a house on the lake in North Carolina and invited us all to the house once to go waterskiing. But Dale didn't go out on the boat; he fished instead. So I'd come by him waterskiing while he was sitting out there fishing and splash him with my skis and he laughed, especially when I caught a tip and busted my ass!

My friend Trudi Stalker shot this photo in Victory Circle at the Indianapolis Motor Speedway, when Dale Earnhardt won the Brickyard 400 in 1995, after qualifying 13th. Everybody was so happy when he won that race. Dale was happy too but he looks like a deer in the headlights right here. It looks like his wife Theresa is poking me with the checkered flag here, but we were just celebrating!

He caught some fish and asked me if I could cook. I said, "Can you fish?" I cooked the fish for him and made hushpuppies. The next morning he asked if I could make biscuits and I just looked at him and said, "Shut up, come back in a half hour."

I made him some hot homemade biscuits, ham and gravy, grits, and he said, "Damn! Somebody oughta marry you!"

I replied, "Nooooo, I'm paying for a divorce right now. I'm not getting married!" They all teased me.

We stayed friends all along. We made a special shifter for him because he liked his shifter loose. I knew he was going to be a superhero, and when he won his first race in Atlanta I was at the drag races in Florida, so Mother and cousin Billie were at the race with Dale.

Dale won and I flew up to the race and we all went to dinner that night, and he wore his cowboy hat. Then we went over to Booper's house. That was his first win and we spent it with him. Mother stepped into Victory Circle with him and slipped and he caught her. Everyone thought that was his mother; it was in the papers. He stayed real close with Mother through the years. We loved Dale; he was really special and his crash was one of the most devastating things to happen, not just to me but to racing all over the world.

Sanctioning Some Sand

The first NASCAR-sanctioned race was held on the sand at Daytona Beach (actually, half the track was on the beach and the other half was Highway A1A, with corners connecting them). Atlanta's Red Byron won it in a modified Ford. Just six days later, NASCAR was officially incorporated.

At first, it had three main classes of cars, but the most popular quickly became the stock class, with stock four-door family sedans that were raced against each other in completely factory-stock trim. Basically, they could change tires and oil, and that was about it. NASCAR called the class Grand National.

Jim Roper of Great Bend, Kansas, won the first Grand National race, held at the Charlotte, North Carolina, fairgrounds on June 19, 1949. The crowd

"The first decade for the NASCAR Grand National series was one of tremendous growth. Characters became heroes and fans hung on every turn of the wheel, watching drivers manhandle cars at speeds fans wished they could legally run themselves."

was huge and they loved watching the same style of cars that they had sitting out in the parking lot duke it out door handle to door handle on the track.

As NASCAR says, "The first decade for the NASCAR Grand National series was one of tremendous growth. Characters became heroes and fans hung on every turn of the wheel, watching drivers manhandle cars at speeds fans wished they could legally run themselves." Over the years, the Grand National class morphed into the Winston Cup (when tobacco company R. J. Reynolds became the series' primary sponsor). It eventually became today's Sprint Cup Series.

Building Daytona

To make the racing faster and easier to watch, Mr. France built Daytona International Speedway in 1959. The paved track's high-banked corners let the cars go much faster. With grandstands, the people got a better look at the

That's my baby Davey Allison when he won the Daytona 500 in 1992. That's his daddy, Bobby, on the right, also a Daytona 500 winner, and his mother, Judy, with team owner Robert Yates on the far right. We were in Victory Circle and Davey had his baby in his hands when it pooped its diapers, and he said, "Aunt Linda, take the baby!" So he handed it to me, and I handed it to his momma. Oh, we were so happy.

At the bottom left of this photo you can see that this was one of Jeff Gordon's five wins at the Brickyard 400! He's the only five-time winner at Indianapolis. This is in Victory Circle, when I took my nephews Sean Vaughn and Mike Padgett up on the podium. Not many people get to go up on the podium like that. Thank you Nancy George! (Tom Siefker Photo)

action. But Daytona is much more than just a racetrack. It has its own aura, its own personality. I love going to any race there, from the 500 to the 24 Hours of Daytona and even the motorcycle races, which I've been to a few times.

I've only missed one Daytona 500, when I was going through my divorce, but Mother went and represented me. It killed me to miss that race, but at least a Vaughn lady was there!

We were in Nancy George's motorhome at the Brickyard 400 and got stuck in it, so they had to come unlock it and let us out. It was parked right next to King Richard's motorhome, so he came to see what the fuss was all about and I got this picture with him. (Photo Courtesy Tom Siefker)

With Richard Petty again, at The Chart House in Daytona, for dinner. That's my friend Trudi Stalker on the left.

Ken Schrader was also at the Goodyear signing. They don't say "tire" down in Alabama, they say "taaaar."

This was in Gasden, Alabama, during Talladega Week. It's a full week of festivities and they ran me around all over the place. I was at the Goodyear plant and this guy won a race tire so I signed it for him.

This is at Atlanta Motor Speedway with Linda Petty, Wanda Lund, Doris Roberts, and my other girls before the start of Richard Petty's last race. What a day that was. The King went out in style but also had a big fire, so we weren't really happy about how the race ended, but all of us girls were there for him. Mother was with me that day, but she's not in this photo. She's probably down in the pits with Richard!

That's my baby, Tony Stewart. I love Tony. If I were younger, he'd be in trouble; the whole world knows that! I watched him grow up, racing his go-karts when he was eight years old, and then he went on to do some Indy testing for A. J. Foyt. I used to joke with him that he was A. J.'s illegitimate child. Whenever I could, I'd ask A. J., "This is the one you didn't tell me about, huh, A. J.?"

That's my boy Tony, at Daytona with Trudi Stalker.

I realize that this photo is of poor quality, but it's a very important one to include here. From left to right are Nancy George, Courtney Hansen, Tony Stewart, and I, at the Brickyard 400 in 2015.

I was sitting on the couch talking to the girls when Tony sat down next to me, put his arm around me and said, "Alright LV, here's the deal. I think I ought to quit." He had made his decision to retire, but hadn't told anyone at this point.

I told him, "You don't have to prove anything to anybody because you've won championships and you're loved. I think you should do a farewell tour next year to say goodbye to all your fans, and put all the money and proceeds into your mother's foundation, then go on and be a car owner."

Then to lighten the mood and make him smile, I asked him, "Are you really A. J. Foyt's illegitimate child?" Tony and I have a rapport like no other. He's really special to me. (Tom Siefker Photo)

Tony and I on the grid at the Brickyard 400. Right before he got in the car I gave him his Pocket Angel and told him, "I think you're going to win this race today." He did indeed win and afterward we went down and he still had the angel in his pocket.

Tony won the Brickyard 400 twice, in 2005 and 2007, and the 2005 race was Mother's last race. I lost her after that, but she left the Indianapolis Motor Speedway as happy as a lark.

Probably my best memory of her at the Brickyard 400 was one year when the night before the race, we went downtown to St. Elmo's for dinner and took a limo. Dale Earnhardt always sat in the window by the front door at St. Elmo's, and when he saw Mother was getting out of the car, he came running out the front door and helped her up off the curb. Everybody was watching and she shut the door on me! Just goes to show who the queen of the ball was that night: Mother! (Tom Siefker Photo)

Robby Gordon, our California boy. I love Robby. This was the last NASCAR race he ran at Indianapolis. Robby was his own worst enemy in NASCAR but he was good. Robby was a great IndyCar driver, and an off-road racer personified. When he ran out of gas leading the Indy 500 in 1999, with barely one lap left, I cried so hard. I threw up that night because I was so sad for him. The telemetry shouldn't have let him lose that race.

" Linda Vaughn is racing royalty, no matter whether it's at the U.S. Nationals, Indy 500, Daytona 500, the Rolex 24, or any other race. Everybody knows who Linda Vaughn is. There is hardly anybody in racing who can walk into anyone's trailer at any time to say hi without getting a dirty look. Linda is the one person who can do that because she knows everyone and gets along with everyone. She is good for the sport and a great ambassador. **"**

— Tony Stewart

This was in the winner's circle at the Daytona 500 when Bobby Allison won. In front are Shelley Harmon Bell, Miss Winston, and me holding the flag, with Bobby right behind me, Bud Moore on the left in the hat and glasses, and the Unocal Race Stoppers with Bobby. (Photo Courtesy International Motor Racing Research Center's National Speed Sport News Collection)

The car is a Hurst Oldsmobile and that's my cousin Billie Whitener hanging out of the door. I sat on top of it. She was married to my cousin and she and I were like sisters. She went to races with me a lot and I'd put her to work. I needed help at the track and said, "We'll pay you if you work," and she did. I had Hurst girls everywhere!

This is Bob Slack, one of the brothers that ran the track at Cayuga International Speedway in Ontario, Canada. It was a 5/8-mile track that started life as a dirt track but was paved in 1967 when the NASCAR stock cars got too fast for the dirt track. Dale Earnhardt, Bobby Allison, Benny Parsons, Dick Trickle, and other big name drivers won at Cayuga.

Here I am with Felix Sabates at the Brickyard. Felix sponsored Robby Gordon in IndyCar when they should have won. Felix and I were both nervous wrecks and were glad it was over; one of the few times I was glad a race was over. Felix told me one time, "Linda, you're a beautiful woman in this business and it's tough. I admire you for hanging in there as long as you have. Most smart women don't last anywhere near as long as you. I congratulate you." I took that as a great compliment coming from such a successful entrepreneur as Felix. I adore Felix Sabates.

My friend Trudi shot this photo of Jack Roush and me. Jack was a drag racer when I met him, partnered with Wayne Gapp, and he was a friend of George Hurst's. Gapp and Roush would be over at the Hurst trailer getting parts all the time. I thought he was smart and we've stayed friends all these years. I'm very proud of him and his daughter Susan, who also drag races.

Trudi and I with Austin Dillon. He and his brother Ty are the grandsons of Richard Childress, but he's earned his ride. He was Rookie of the Year in the Camping World Truck Series (in 2010), won the Truck championship the next year, then won the Nationwide championship in 2013.

Rusty Wallace was one of my mother's favorites. Rusty and I got put into the Die Cast Hall of Fame together in 2015. This photo was shot at the 2014 Performance Racing Industry (PRI) trade show, in C&R Radiators' booth. (Tom Siefker Photo)

Tiny Lund won Daytona when I was Miss Firebird, and they made this board to commemorate it at the 2014 Daytona 500. Here I'm showing it to my cousin Mousie. His name is James Caylor, but we call him Mousie because he's a rat and we love him. He's a big part of racing and everybody knows him. He terrorizes everyone, a big part of the whole racing family.

Trudi and I with Rick Crawford at a Craftsman Truck race at Daytona. During the race before this one he had flipped over and ended up on all four Goodyear tires right in front of the Goodyear suite. I told everyone within earshot in the suite, "Boy those tires sure do work!" Crawford drove for a good friend of mine, Tom Mitchell, from Odessa, Texas, who also had Indy cars. Watching Rick, his style, his finesse, his perseverance, sure was fun. And his good looks didn't bother me at all.

" Think about these important words: icon, ambassador, legend, special, product spokesperson, hall of famer. A true friend is Linda Vaughn.

"I grew up in Mobile Alabama racing short tracks along the gulf coast and then all over the nation. You had to have the best parts to be successful, and one of the best parts I used in every racing machine was a Hurst Shifter.

"I went to the PRI show in Indy about 20 years ago and there Ms. Vaughn was, signing autographs and selling Hurst Shifters. The line waiting for a signature was around the RCADome. But I waited. And let me tell you, it was worth it. I was within five folks of getting a signature, wearing my Circle Bar Race Team jacket, when she noticed me.

"Linda stood up and came over to me with a hug around my neck and a kiss on the cheek and everybody in line thought I was somebody, when the real celebrity is Linda. She knew Tom Mitchell from the Indy Car days back in the early 1980s and now I was his new driver.

"From then on, we had a special relationship and we always were in touch. We also knew the same folks from Dalton, Georgia. If you wanted a showstopper, a room lit up and brought to life, or a person to just make your day even brighter, Linda is your person. She always has the personality, smile, kindness, and is the total package. I'm so proud to have met her and been friends more than 20 years. "

— Rick Crawford

These shots were for a poster we did with Carl Miskotten and his son Carlie. They had a NASCAR team in the early 1990s and lived in Franklin, Tennessee, and had an auction business. Carl is a wonderful, very religious man, and Carlie was a real special boy. It tore me up when he met a very untimely death in Daytona, but it wasn't in a race. He died in a motorcycle accident, on the way back to his condo. We shot this poster with his car in Franklin. That was a great day in my life.

" I first met Linda Vaughn while I was running USAC races in the 1980s. Ann and I were friends with A. J. Foyt, Tim Delrose, and Blackie Fortune, who introduced us to Linda. Because we were within her circle of friends, we too were adopted. When I was at Indianapolis as a rookie in 1983, driving for Usona and Hilda Purcell, our paths crossed again. Her down-to-earth spirit is always the same, she's your friend and she makes you feel special the moment she sees you!

"My racing career took us down South and it was wonderful to see Linda, a familiar face, in the garage area. In 1989, we won the Busch Clash, the pole for the 500, and a Twin 125. To add to all that excitement, we're in Victory Lane and who is there to congratulate us? Linda Vaughn! Wow, that was special. Two of my favorite girls, my wife Ann and Linda, kissing me on the cheek. Every time I see the photo, I am reminded of this career highlight!

"Even now, whenever we see Linda at a racing function, we pick up exactly where we left off; as if no time has passed.

"Linda Vaughn is an icon to all racers and will forever be Miss Hurst for generations of us. "

— Ken Schrader

Ken Schrader is precious and wonderful! He is a real Saturday night racer to me. He can drive on any track on Saturday then come race the big 500-milers on Sunday. Ken is one fine, great competitor and is still racing. He's the kind of person that you can run door-handle-to-door-handle with at 200 mph and you know you're safe. A true gentleman racer. He and his wife have a huge collection of Chevrolets. (Brian Cleary Photo)

Here we are with another one of the Allisons, this time Donnie, in Victory Circle at the Firecracker 400. From left to right are Miss Firecracker 400, Banjo Mathews, me, Donnie Allison, and Miss Unocal. Donnie had one fast car thanks to Banjo. We called Donnie "BJ" and we always carried Rolaids for him because his stomach was always in knots. He'd say, "Hey honey, you got a Rolaids?" Donnie was great. (Photo Courtesy Smyle Media)

Here I am in Victory Circle at the Daytona 500 with upset-winner Earl Balmer. That's Miss Ingersoll-Rand on the left and Tim Sullivan in the back left with the glasses. Tim was a promotional man for Valvoline, Daytona, Ingersoll-Rand, and others and he and Jack Duffy worked well together.

Advance Auto Parts was a big outlet, a warehouse distributor for Hurst, so we did a lot of promotions at racetracks like this one.

I first met Troy Aikman, the quarterback of the Dallas Cowboys, at the Daytona 500. The first thing I noticed were his boots, then my eyes went up to his face and I was, "Hi there." Troy was a good friend of Sterling Marlin's. This photo was in Texas at Billy Meyer's track. When he came up to me and said, "Don't I know you?"

The Daytona 500 in 1981, with Phil Harsh. Phil pitted with Bobby Wawak's Buick (that was driven by Henry Jones from Kansas). The eye injury was suffered in the pits when a metal fragment hit him. It was removed two days later in Charlotte.

"The saddest was when we lost him. [Dale Earnhardt] That bump going into Turn 4 worries me. I just hope it ain't one of my boys that hits it. That bump was what killed him."

Daytona Memories

My best and worst memories of Daytona both involve Dale Earnhardt. The best memory was when Dale finally won. I felt it in my gut that morning that he was going to win that race. And he did.

The whole place, every mechanic on every team walked to the pit line as he came in and he got a standing ovation from not just the fans in the stands, but from the entire racing world. Everybody was standing up. And Victory Circle was wild! There were security people all over the place. The security was tight but of course I had the credential to go everywhere. But instead of joining him, I stood off to the side while he was on the podium, and it was some of the best eye contact I ever had with Dale. It was sensational, just sharing it with him. I was real proud, real happy.

The saddest was when we lost him. That morning we all went to our motorsports church, and after church I walked back to the car to do my makeup and an announcer walked up to Dale to do a live interview, so I listened to the interview from the car. Dale said, "Well if I don't win today I hope one of my boys do" and then I remember him saying, "That bump going into Turn 4 worries me. I just hope it ain't one of my boys that hits it." As we were leaving he walked by and brushed up against me, gave me that smile of his, and walked to his car.

That bump was what killed him. I was up in the Goodyear suite watching the race and saw that crash by the bump and knew it was Dale. I got in the car immediately and left and went to the hospital and saw them bring him in, and I knew he was dead. He wore his seatbelts real loose, like he liked his shifter, and the impact just snapped his neck.

I went back to the hotel and waited and waited, and Mother called and asked, "Linda how is he?"

I said he passed and she said, "They haven't announced a thing, not a thing."

I told her, "They won't because there will be a riot. They won't announce it until way after dark, sugar."

That morning Dale had said that if he couldn't win then he hoped one of team's boys did. And they finished 1st and 2nd: Michael Waltrip won and (Dale) Junior took 2nd for him. When they told Waltrip in Victory Circle that Dale was dead, it was so bittersweet. I couldn't be a part of it; I had to get out of there and that's why I went back to the hotel. That was probably the darkest day of my life at Daytona so I chose to be by myself.

They finally came on and Mike Helton, bless his heart, had the responsibility to announce to the world that Dale Earnhardt had died. That was around 8:00 pm that night. I was sick all day, crying.

A lot of people tried to say that Sterling Marlin touched Dale in the back and that's what caused the wreck, but Kenny Schrader was right on him and said, "No one bumped him. It was the bump in the track that took Dale's life."

People also blamed Bill Simpson for supplying faulty safety harnesses, and NASCAR threw him under the bus. But those seat belts were cut and I saw it, and I stood up for Bill Simpson because he did *not* make something that was faulty. They were cut and there was a cover-up, and I think the whole world knows that now.

Bill Simpson and Dale were great pals, really great buddies and very, very close. If it hadn't been for Bill Simpson, my legs would have been burnt off at every racetrack in the United States and Europe. Ethanol at the Speedway doesn't have a color when it burns, and if I hadn't worn Bill Simpson's uniforms I would have been parched many times. I told him, "When you get to Indianapolis, there's going to be a whole different story. You just hang in there," and I saw him come out of the NASCAR rig that morning and smile at me, I knew that he had finally been heard.

And thank God for Tony George and all the people who knew and loved Bill Simpson for all that he did for this sport. I lost two of my loves in racing to freak accidents and the truth be known, it had to take our most popular driver for safety to advance to where it is today. That track's fixed now. And they have restraints and HANS devices now, just better equipment in general. But what a dark day at Daytona and a dark day for the world.

A NASCAR Day

The NASCAR audience was fabulous. I spent a lot of time going to the Living Legends autograph sessions, fan fares, and the like with all the guys including Petty, Pearson, and Cale. When the International Race of Champions (IROC) series was created (with the help of Hurst), the NASCAR audience was there too. NASCAR fans are unbelievable, very dedicated. They grew up with it, and passed it down to their children. We now have three generations of fans.

As Miss Firebird, all of my duties were NASCAR-related plus a couple of TV promotions. I visited cities for the Pure Oil Company and made personal appearances with a number of the drivers. When the teleprompter came on the scene, we promoted the first telecast of the Daytona 500. It was a whole big promotion to bring live TV to Daytona.

When I retired as Miss Firebird and became Miss Hurst Golden Shifter in 1966, I was traveling three times as much, going to 134 events in a year. I took what I learned as Miss Firebird and applied it to what I saw George Hurst needed to do in NASCAR and also Indianapolis, and put it all together to run three circuits (with drag racing as well). I was the busiest girl I've ever seen. No home life for me; honey, I was constantly on the road. My pad was a suitcase and my true love was getting to go to all the races.

Starting in 1966, I attended all the major 500-mile NASCAR races, all the major IndyCar races, off-road races like the Baja 1000, and every one of the NHRA races. There were 134 events a year, sometimes two or three a week, plus the Armed Forces events in between, then things like the *Hemi Under Glass* (that would be on a Wednesday and Thursday), and then Friday you're at the race all weekend. Then you're making sure your product is working right, doing seminars, going to press conferences, trade shows, and then there were rain-outs so we'd try to bring the show inside. We formed a few more trade shows; it was all very strenuous.

Those were the days when you could change your flights easily when you needed to be flexible. Now, you'd have a heck of a time changing flights like we did. The cost of everything now is just unbelievable. When I worked for Hurst, we had our own travel agency that handled my travel. I worked with a girl named Carolyn who did all the booking for me. Jack Duffy and I would have staff meetings and go over everything and plan ahead. We were pretty organized because we had to line up the trucks, the parade cars, girls and costumes (which were my departments), setting up radio, and TV shows. It was a full time job, all the time. I was honestly married to racing!

TLR my superstar! Timothy Larry Richmond, TLR. This was during one of his NASCAR races, and I still have that uniform in my house. I had a very special relationship with TLR that I'm not going to get into. Suffice it to say that we loved each other deeply, and I miss him every day. This photo of him in street clothes . . . he was trying to sweet-talk me into something that night. He was so good looking and had a way with women. Damn.

6 | THE INDY 500

Back in Chapter 2, I talked about nearly being killed in a balloon at the Indianapolis Motor Speedway. Most people don't know that the very first official race at the Speedway was in fact a hot air balloon race, on June 5, 1909, two years before what we now know as the Indianapolis 500.

Page 139: Jack Duffy took this photo at the Pocono race with A. J., June, and me, and those are Duffy's kids in the background. I absolutely thought that A. J. was the best-looking race car driver; he had the prettiest teeth. He has a great big foot and a big heart, and that's more important. June and I used to absolutely terrorize him and he loved it!

A. J. invited us to his open house at his dealership after this race and I ordered a Cadillac from him. I made sure several of my friends that wanted a Cadillac ordered it through A. J.'s dealership.

The balloon race was followed in August of that year with some motorcycle races and then the first actual automobile race on August 19, 1909. The 100-lap Prest-O-Lite Trophy was won by Bob Burman in a Buick.

The 2.5-mile oval Speedway was built that year by Indiana businessmen Carl G. Fisher, James A. Allison, Arthur C. Newby, and Frank H. Wheeler, who put their money together to build the track as an automotive testing facility to help support the growing automobile industry in Indiana and all over the Midwest. To put things into perspective about how long ago 1909 really was are these facts: William Howard Taft was the President; the National Association for the Advancement of Colored People (NAACP) was formed; Robert Peary, Matthew Henson, and four Native explorers reached the North Pole; and construction began on the RMS *Titanic*. Yes, the Indianapolis Motor Speedway has been around that long.

Initially, the racetrack was paved with gravel and tar, but that was replaced the next year with 3.2 million bricks, which is why the Speedway is commonly referred to as "The Brickyard," as in NASCAR's Brickyard 400. The first winner of the "International 500-Mile Sweepstakes Race," as it was called back then

In the very early days of my career, women we not allowed in the pits at the Indianapolis 500, so Dottie Parker and I were fence hangers this year.

Few things say Indianapolis 500 like the name A. J. Foyt. I'm pretty sure this was in 1966 when A. J. won the award for taking the pole position. I love A. J. and we're still great friends, although we love to give each other a hard time whenever we can. Putting me in a top hat and tails was George Hurst's idea, so Mother made the outfit for me.

This is Jim Haines, a longtime photographer for Speedway. As far as we can tell, he was a freelance photographer who spent a lot of time at Indy, but I don't think he was ever on the payroll.

Here is a gang of players. From left to right are Dale Drake (of Drake Engines), Sid Collins, Tony Hulman (of the Hulman family that still owns the Indianapolis Motor Speedway), me, and June Cochran.

This is Roger McClusky at an IndyCar race in Phoenix; he was from Tucson. Roger was a star of the United States Auto Club (USAC), winning sprint car and stock car titles, and he also raced in IndyCars like here in Phoenix. He was in the Indy 500 18 times and finished a best of 3rd. He also drove one of the Ford/Holman-Moody GT40s at Le Mans.

With the famous Lloyd Ruby and J. C. Agajanian in Gasoline Alley; I want to say 1967 or 1968. Lloyd rode his motorcycle into Gasoline Alley that day. He raced in the Indianapolis 500 18 times, from 1960 to 1977 with a best finish of 3rd in 1964, but he should have won four times. He never quite got it.

Al Unser was quoted as saying that Lloyd was his hero, "He was honest and a hard racer. He didn't pull things on you. You could run wheel-to-wheel with him and you didn't have to worry about Lloyd. He made the race car talk." Lloyd passed away in 2009 and we just put him into the Hall of Fame a few years ago. He and J. C. Agajanian were both my big brothers.

Lloyd called me his "little siiiii-ister." He talked real slow. Do you know why I made them my brothers? Because we had a special relation-ship and they would never hit on me, like so many other people did.

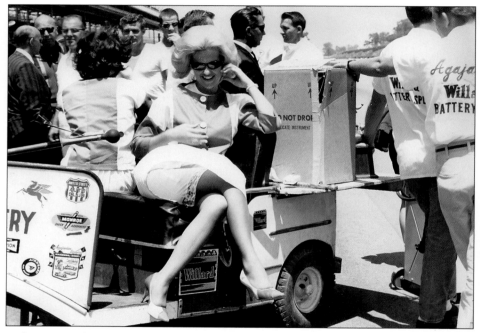

Relaxing in the pits at Indy, in timing and scoring, with the Agajanian crew. That's Booper sitting on the golf cart with her back to the camera, talking to all the men of course!

Dean Moon gave me this shirt at the Indianapolis 500 so I stood up and took a picture with it.

" Beautiful, blond, sexy; Linda Vaughn is rightly called the "First Lady of Racing." An icon in the NASCAR and drag racing world, she came to Indianapolis in the early 1960s and half a century later she is still there enjoying her friendships with drivers, young and old, as well as the Hulman Family.

"Linda in white boots and flowing beauty queen costume, rolling about on top of the pace car, and waving to cheering fans in the stands became every bit as much a cherished Indy 500 tradition as Jim Nabors on the podium singing "Back Home Again in Indiana." Her provoking, eye-catching appearance often masked her hard work behind the scenes for corporate sponsor Hurst whose spokeswoman she became.

"She was a friend to many, a confidante to some, and a mother hen to all who needed a kind word or a shoulder to cry on. In a world of tough men, Linda remained a Southern lady, feisty, indomitable, and brave, the twinkle in her eyes ever ready to sparkle.

"When we occasionally run into each other nowadays at a car event here and there we reminisce about the good old Indy 500 days; as only old-timers can, who, in Chris Economaki's immortal words, know "what it was like out there." Linda did; she is a survivor. "

— Dan Gurney

Daniel Gurney and I at Indianapolis Motor Speedway, both dressed in our Goodyear colors. We made some appearances together over the years. We first met at the Riverside Grand Prix, when he was running road courses. He was so handsome. Then he came to Indianapolis and of course I watched everything going on at Indy. It was a very close group there. Through Hurst Airheart, we worked very closely with Dan on his Eagle race cars so I've known him through his whole career, and watched his kids grow up. The kids are racing now (I just saw them at the Indianapolis 500 in 2015) and Dan and his wife Effie still stay in touch with me.

This is Jimmy Endervite, the chief engineer for Lola, and John Mecom, who owned the car. They brought the car to the Speedway in 1966 and brought Graham Hill to Indianapolis from Formula 1 to drive it, the first Formula 1 racer at Indy. And they won. Mecom had another Lola entered in that same race, driven by Sir Jackie Stewart.

This is when I drug A. J. out to the drags at the U.S. Nationals in Indianapolis, and we were sitting in Snake's pit watching them change the engine. Snake was tickled to death that I brought the great A. J. Foyt to the dragstrip. A. J. loved drag racing, but I still had to lure him.

The Indianapolis 500 in 1972, where I had the great pleasure of presenting a 1972 Hurst Oldsmobile W30 big-block 455 to Mark Donohue on the stage and gave him a great big kiss in front of God, Roger Penske, and everybody. As you can see, Junebug was a little bit jealous because she had a bit of a crush on Mark too, but that's okay because we were the best of friends. And we loved him dearly.

Mark and I became very close and wonderful friends. And when he told me he wanted to do the IROC series, Hurst jumped on board right away. In this photo, June's a little ticked off because he was talking strategy with me and I was really into him, and June was pouting, "Hey, what about meeee? Mark confided in us and that was fabulous. I admired him. Everybody did. He was such a sweet, unassuming quiet engineer. Brilliant man.

This was also at the Pocono IndyCar race, with June and I playing around with Mario Andretti. Mario always picked on Junebug and, as you can see, she's really embarrassed. I'm not going to tell you what he said!

Mario, after he won Michigan a few years later, with me holding the trophy. This race was on a really hot summer day, and man what a race Mario had on his hands with Rick Mears and A. J.! Winning that day was one fine accomplishment for Mario.

“ The only other person who exudes as much charisma as Linda Vaughn is Marilyn Monroe. Linda has a charm that attracts people. And I never saw anyone more voluptuous and glamourous at a racetrack than Linda. She is like artistry in pit lane. Men draw an audible breath. Some men try to look down, but of course don't.

"But don't get the wrong idea.

"Linda has always been a special lady. Wisely, she made herself more than a blonde sex symbol presence in Victory Lane. She represents companies with glamour and style, takes part in charity events and parades and other automotive events. She can be found on race weekends interacting with fans, sponsors, and drivers and their wives and families.

"It isn't only the men who like her. Women like her, too. You notice her looks first, but then realize that she has a lot of class, a great personality, and there is a genuine kindness about her.

"She is always very professional and that's why she has had longevity. She knows the sport well, which allows her to fit in. She knows all the different race disciplines. She speaks intelligently, even about the technical side. She takes a lot of responsibility for the role she has been allowed to sustain for so many decades.

"I've known Linda since 1963 and it is still a pleasure to see her. She remains to this day gracious, generous, and beautiful; and living a rock star life. I guess the icons I remember are not all drivers. ”

— Mario Andretti

This was at the Budweiser Cleveland Grand Prix with Paul Newman. We all stayed downtown in this beautiful old re-done hotel and Mario invited us to dinner with Bill Yeager (the Clown Prince of racing we called him; he called himself a gofer) who took care of Paul Newman and worked with all the greats too, Carl Haas, Carl's wife, Bernie, me, and Paul Newman.

The Father, a devout Catholic, took this picture and got Paul to sign it for me; he never autographs anything so I was elated, floating on clouds.

One time we were at Indianapolis talking just like this and I said, "Just think about all those people behind us and what they must be thinking," and Paul turned and dipped me and acted like he was kissing me, and I threw my hands back. That whole grandstand went crazy. It was so hilarious. They probably started rumors, but we were just great friends.

His wife, Joanne Woodward, who is a Southerner too, once told me, "I hate to love you, but I love to hate you."

And I said, "Well which is it?"

And she said, "We love you."

Paul and I always wanted to do a movie together and talked about it a lot, but we could never get a script. He said, "If we ever get a decent script I know just the part you could play. We'll get it done." But we never got it done.

You can see from his casualness how fond of each other we were.

Every year in the month of May at Indianapolis Motor Speedway, they have a bicycle race called The Little 500. A whole bunch of drivers are in the race. In this photo, that's Gary Bettenhausen on the bike. I was his relief driver: He rode the first part and I rode the second part and we won!

At Indianapolis with the 1979 Ford Mustang pace car, with Shelley Harmon Bell on the driver's door. Mother made those outfits, of course, and mine was the only one with the hole cut out of it.

Albert Unser Sr. is my brother and I named Little Al my nephew. Al and I were very close and did some television shows together with John Denver. Al was going to be the next four-time winner of the Indianapolis 500, but he didn't have a ride that month. I told him to get that Cummins car and he'd kick everyone's butt. He got the ride at the last minute, from Roger Penske, and I told him before the race, "You're going to win this one brother."

When I saw him in Victory Circle he hugged and kissed me. We were thrilled to death. I knew that car and I knew him, and I told him he'd win. I never say that unless I really believe it. That was his fourth win, making him one of four four-time winners of the Indianapolis 500.

Daniel Ezekiel Ongais, my mother's Hawaiian boyfriend. I knew Danny of course from his drag racing days but he came to race at the Indianapolis 500, where this photo was taken, in 1979.

He about gave me a heart attack in 1981 when he crashed very hard in Turn 3. He lost control and went head-on into the wall at darn near 200 mph and it tore the entire front end off the car, and left his legs dangling on the track while he slid to a stop. The worst picture in my mind was looking out and seeing his legs dangling out of the car. He was airlifted to the hospital and we all thought the worst, but he came out of it with a concussion and two broken legs.

It took years of rehab and operations from Doctor Corcoran to recover, and I visited him many times in the hospital. The last time I saw Danny was when he came to the Motorsports Hall of Fame ceremony. It's always an honor to see all of those guys every year.

Chip Ganassi circa 1982 or 1983 (left) and now (below). Chip got started at Indianapolis in 1982 when he graduated with a finance degree from Duquesne, and he ran the Indianapolis 500 five times, with a best finish of 8th. I was very proud to have helped Chip get started and he and I are like brother and sister, and have always confided in each other; we're in each other's world. He's a true angel brother of mine. Of course he's a great entrepreneur and now one of the most successful team owners in the history of racing.

I was Chip's guest at the 2015 24 Hours of Daytona, which his team won, and the next week I was going to the Motorsports Hall of Fame and Chip was my date. I thought I was going to be a presenter for the Living Legends of NASCAR award, but I was actually nominated and given the award, and Chip was the presenter. He gave the same speech that he gave at my roast at the Lucas Estate in Indianapolis the year before, and it was so special, so sweet. NASCAR Vice Chairman Mike Helton was there, so were the Allisons . . . there wasn't a dry eye in the place. I'm getting inducted into all these halls of fame. I hope I'm going to be around next year to see what's next. I'm not through yet folks!

" The top photo was taken at a Super Vee race in Michigan. Linda was always helping young drivers, introducing them to industry executives. I was no exception. She made calls for me throughout my Formula Ford and Super Vee days and I often ask myself why.

"She was just a great woman who always wanted to help, even if I was a no-name driver at that point in my career.

Still, today, like at this NASCAR event, Linda's always there to listen, give advice, or just be a friend. Never in the way, always gracious to the other women, and always welcome on teams around the Paddock Area of Formula 1, to the Garage Area in Indianapolis, to the Pit Lane of Daytona. "

— Chip Ganassi

Tim Richmond, when he qualified for the Indy 500 in 1980. I told him he was going to be the Rookie of the Year, and he was. His Indy race was probably best known for the ride back to the pits. Tim ran out of gas on the last lap and was still with his car when Johnny Rutherford was taking his victory lap. On the way to the pits, Johnny stopped and gave Tim a ride on the sidepod of his IndyCar, all the way back to the winner's circle.

The crowd went nuts and I was just gushing with pride. You can see by the look in my eyes how much I truly loved Tim Richmond.

This is Booper and I with Jim Hurtubise, who was such a great showman at the Speedway. He had one of the worst fires I've ever seen (in Milwaukee) that took most of his fingers on one hand. When his doctors asked him how he wanted his damaged hands shaped permanently, Jim said, "Just make 'em so I can hold a steering wheel."

He raced in the Indianapolis 500 up until 1974 with his hands like that. Due to that accident, he helped save the lives of a lot of people with the safety standards they applied afterward.

My favorite memory of Jim was when he brought the Novi car to Indy and they wouldn't let him run it, so he filled the cockpit full of beer and gave it to all the fans. Like I said, he was a real showman. Jim died of a heart attack in 1989, when he was 56 years old. (Photo Courtesy Meeka Cook)

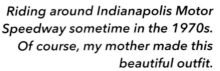

Riding around Indianapolis Motor Speedway sometime in the 1970s. Of course, my mother made this beautiful outfit.

The lady in the black shirt was a promoter and track owner in Australia. When she came to the United States she wanted to meet James Garner, who was driving the pace car for us at the Indy 500. So Booper (yellow shirt) and I introduced her to Garner and took this picture. (Photo Courtesy Meeka Cook)

This is Booper and I with Bill Neely, who wrote A. J.'s book. Bill used to be the Public Relations Director for Goodyear and Booper really liked him. The three of us formed the Bear Club. That's Neely Bear, Linda Bear, and Betty Bear. (Photo Courtesy Meeka Cook)

and run on the bricks in 1911, was Ray Harroun in a Marmon Wasp (which is still on display in the Speedway's fantastic museum in the infield).

The original group of businessmen owners sold the track to World War I ace pilot Eddie Rickenbacker in 1927 and when World War II broke out, Rickenbacker closed the track and it fell into disrepair, with weeds growing through the bricks and the grandstands nearly falling down. Indiana businessman Tony Hulman Jr. bought the Speedway after the war ended in 1945, and it remains in his family today. In 1989, Mr. Hulman's only grandson, Tony Hulman George, took over as president and CEO of the track.

Tony Hulman George is the man responsible for building the infield road course, as well as bringing NASCAR, Formula 1, and MotoGP

James Garner

One of the greatest promotional ventures I ever had was when I asked Jim Garner to drive the pace car at the Indianapolis 500. He was fighting with the studios at the time. They hadn't renewed his contract for *The Rockford Files* and I said, "Jim, I have a great idea and we'll pay you and take care of your expenses. Drive the 1977 Oldsmobile pace car at the 500 and stuff it up the studio's butt, because that's the number-one publicity stunt in the world. I guarantee you'll get your contract."

And it worked; they realized what they had and he got five years on *Rockford*. He came to Indianapolis about 20 years straight, and he was wonderful. I was so honored and proud to be a part of that. I miss Jim.

The first time I met Jim was at Ensenada, Mexico, for the Baja 1000 and he was driving the Hurst *Baja Boot* Oldsmobile. Of course everyone knew who he was, and he came up to me and said, "Are you Linda Vaughn?" He shook my hand and said, "I'm gonna drive this shitbox here, I hope it stays together. Are you going to fly in the spotter plane and look out for me?"

I was in the plane with the pilot and George Hurst. He did well. He broke down one time and that's when I got into one of the chase vehicles to ride back to Ensenada and it about beat me to death. I had to duct tape my boobs in place because it was so bouncy.

Jim won class and we spent time at La Paz and it developed into a great friendship. Then the next year he came to Indianapolis and we all got to spend time together. Danny Folsom, the chicken king, had a big party at his house. He was a friend of Peter Revson and we brought Garner. I wore a white dress and they threw me into the pool that night. I'll never forget that. I

Junebug, James Garner, and I at the Speedway on qualifying day.

wouldn't come out until they brought me a towel. Then we all drove back together and got stopped by the police, and he told the cop, "This is why I'm driving so fast, she's soaking wet and cold!"

He was quite the character, very funny, and everybody loved him. He was a great friend and one handsome son of a gun too.

motorcycle races to the track. Before him the only race held at his family's track was the Indy 500. He stepped down from his position of running the track in 2009 and handed it over to others, but the Speedway is still owned by the Hulman George family, and Tony's sister Nancy George is one of my dearest friends to this day.

My first time at the Indianapolis Motor Speedway was in 1963, as Miss Firebird, and it was absolutely breathtaking! The place is enormous. I thought it was like every track rolled into one at one time, and the crowd was the biggest I had ever seen in my life. They estimate that the crowd every year is close to 300,000, which I think makes it the most-attended sporting event in the entire world, and by a long shot. Just going through the tunnel into the infield affects me the same way today as it did that first time.

And when they say, "Gentlemen, start your engines," I'm usually crying and screaming and have goose bumps all over my body. It just affects me in a very spiritual way that is hard to describe, and I can feel the emotion just writing this.

Indianapolis is not all about good times, however. During my second race, in 1964, I sat in the grandstands coming out of Turn 4 onto the front straight, right where Eddie Sachs and Davey McDonald crashed and were killed in a horrible fiery crash. I had just met them both the year before and to lose them both at once was just devastating. It was the worst accident I have ever seen in person at Indianapolis, or anywhere else, and it still haunts me to this day.

King Richard Petty with one of my very best friends, Nancy George, and I at the Indianapolis Motor Speedway. Nancy is Tony George's sister, the Indianapolis Motor Speedway family. (Tom Siefker Photo)

❝ When I was a little girl growing up around the track I never dreamed that Linda Vaughn would someday be my best friend! Throughout the years, Linda has not only been an ambassador for all forms of motor racing, she has personally taught me so much about racing, amid the fun we've had!

"She has gotten me out of my shell, as I tend to be quite shy at times. She has taught me to believe in myself and has given me the confidence that only a best friend could give. She's been like a big sister to me and I am proud to call her my best friend. If there's one thing she has, it's your back!

"Her popularity never ceases to amaze me. It's her love of the fans, the ability to never forget a name or a face, her incredible sense of humor, and her genuine love of racing that has made her such a legend. This is something that can't be bought (many think they have it but don't) and it takes years to achieve. She has given me many years of fond memories, wisdom I'll always remember, and fun that I'll always cherish! She keeps me young! Her energy never ceases to amaze me, and her smile is always a pleasure to behold! I love her! ❞

— *Nancy George*

"You can go to work in the morning and have breakfast with your best friends in racing and then go to a funeral home that night."

The smell of burning human flesh is devastating; something you never forget, like the first time you smell a skunk. I'll never forget that smell, and it will always remain embedded in my mind. I was so tragically stressed and screaming and crying and smelling that awful smell, all at the same time, all those senses. I had nightmares about it for years. Like it or not, that's the danger inherent in racing and I understand that, but it never gets easier to see a friend get injured or, God forbid, killed. They both lost their lives right in front of me that day but this goes with my job, unfortunately. You can go to work in the morning and have breakfast with your best friends in racing and then go to a funeral home that night.

It's hard to talk about it, very hard to describe how I feel while writing this. But we learned so much from their deaths, and it took two of our greatest superstars (our clown prince Eddie Sachs, what a great driver and a great, funny man, and Dave McDonald, a quiet, sweet, unassuming, longhaired California boy with the prettiest teeth) to make the cars safer, as they are today. And having the opportunity to work with great men like Bill Simpson and George Hurst with the Hurst Rescue Tool. We lose people to save others.

The next year, Scotland's Jimmy Clark won the race in the rear-engine Lotus with a Ford engine. He led for 190 laps, almost the entire race, and the only other driver to lead a lap was A. J. Foyt, for 10 laps. A. J. started the race on the pole but Jimmy quickly passed him. Jimmy was racing in Formula 1 that year and not only won the Indy 500 but he was also the Formula 1 world champion the same year, which nobody else has ever done.

Jim Clark and I were very close. He was one of the nicest men I've ever had in my life, a gentlemen's gentleman, and we had a true long-distance love affair. Looking back over the years, I have loved several men, but I can honestly say that Jim Clark was the love of my life. His hero was A. J. so when he got to the Speedway the first time, in 1963, of course he wanted to meet A. J. But A. J. was ugly to him. Jim was very shy and came to America to race the great A. J. Foyt and A. J. hurt his feelings. That pissed me off, that A. J. could be such a jerk to such a nice, gentle man.

I cussed A. J. out for that and told him, "A. J., you're going to have to race this boy and he's going to race your ass out of you."

He told me, "Oh, you favor him over me?"

And I said, "I love you both but you're going to have to race him." Then Jimmy whipped his ass.

Jimmy came with the rear-engine Lotus for the first time and it upset a lot of people, including A. J. who was still racing the soon-to-be-obsolete front-engine roadster. But they were ready, Jim, Colin Chapman, and Jim Endervite (their chief mechanic). They were a lovely team of gentlemen and I enjoyed showing them around at night, taking them out to dinner. They were foreigners in our town and I thought it was my place to be nice to them and show them around, so Booper and I took them all out on the town. It was wonderful.

The next year, in 1966, another Formula 1 hero Graham Hill came to Indy to drive for John Mecom and won the 500. My best friend Booper had the biggest crush on Graham Hill. She talked real slow and Graham would say, "I just want to sit here and listen to you two girls talk to me."

The best Indy 500 for me professionally was in 1972. We had my Hurst Oldsmobile as the pace car with my dear friend, the famous and incredibly handsome James Garner, driving it, and my other good friend Mark Donahue winning the race in Roger Penske's car. It was Garner's first time at the race, Mark's only win at Indy, and Roger's first win at the track.

Peter Revson

Peter Revson. What can I say? He's the most gorgeous man that ever walked into the Indianapolis Motor Speedway. I melted when I met him, and only bought Revlon products from then on.

Peter was unique, an aristocrat from New York but shy and quiet, unassuming. Most people never knew about the Revlon connection because he never talked about it, but he was an heir to the Revlon fortune. Jim Clark and I were very close and I loved him so much, that when Peter won the Jim Clark Award, I was so proud to present it to him at the Athletic Club in Indianapolis, and it just opened up a whole new bunch of heartfelt feelings for another race driver. He was so special and I paid attention to him.

He was driving the McLaren and I knew Bruce McLaren well, the whole team really, including Tyler Alexander, the chief mechanic. I said, "Tyler, if he can get through 4."

Tyler said, "He'll get through 4."

So I watched him run the day before qualifying and watched him in Turns 1 and 4, and I was just stoked.

I told him the next morning that he was going to win the pole and he looked at me like, "What?" and then went back to his concentration.

Peter got the pole that day. Afterward, I went over to see him and he said, "Linda Vaughn, you are car and driver." That was one of the greatest compliments anyone has ever paid me in my life.

Peter did well at the Indianapolis 500 but never won. He was angry at some of the politics going on there, so he went to drive for Yardley in Formula 1. I thought it was too sudden but I supported him. He was going to drive the Shadow in F1 and I didn't want him to drive the Shadow. I didn't trust that car at all.

I went snow skiing on March 22, the day he was racing that Shadow in South Africa and got killed. Denny Hulme called and told me that Peter had died, that he'd broken every bone in his body and passed on.

I had never skied a high slope until that day and I was learning how to ski so I could go skiing with Peter. I was really . . . hurt. Devastated. Lost. It took me quite some time to get it together, after losing him.

I have the nicest letter he wrote to me before he went to Formula 1. His sister Jennifer and I stay in touch. We keep the name Revson going everywhere we can. It's amazing how much he's loved all over the world. He was a gentleman's gentleman, and a ladies' gentleman.

Jennifer Revson:

"The first time I met Linda was at Peter's induction into the Motorsports Hall of Fame of America in 1996, when she came as a presenter for Bill "Grumpy" Jenkins, who was also being inducted that year. Naturally, I knew who she was, having seen her from afar at Indy a few times in the 1970s, and because Peter had mentioned her to me, saying the nicest things; mostly about how fun she was, and her uncanny sixth sense.

"It was Linda who told Peter he would get the pole at Indy in 1971. A prediction that was against all odds.

"I was immediately struck by her kindness and sensitive heart. And as I got to know her better, I was impressed by how principled and dedicated she is. She really walks the talk. And lest some people think she's simply a golden bombshell (I mean, looking at her physical attributes has became a national pastime), she's the furthest from a blonde joke you'll ever meet. The woman is street-smart and *very* intentional.

"Through the years we've had a lot of laughs together, during our not-to-be-discussed escapades, and because of our silly sense of humor. I could tell you about all the "children" she's given me in the form of stuffed animals, their names and ages, but that's a book in itself.

"Of course, we've also shared a few tears, mostly over the people we've loved who've passed. I didn't realize it at the time, but she was the one who sent the amazing checkered-flag flower arrangement to the church for Peter's funeral. The card attached read: "My love goes with my champion."

"So for many reasons, Linda will always hold a special place in my heart. The First Lady of Motorsports, she truly is."

ABC's Jack Arute was a great announcer and always treated me fairly. He did quite a few Indy 500s with me and would ask me intelligent questions, whereas some reporters didn't think I knew racing. They were so wrong. I am proud to know Jack Arute.

" The thing about Linda Vaughn is that while on the surface, she was thought of as a 'Beauty Queen,' she was much more! She commanded a legion of fans. Quick with a smile and an encouraging word, Linda became a confidant to many of the sport's famous, and not so famous. Your stature never came into play when Linda was around. She treated everyone the same. Linda became an icon just as significant as Petty, Foyt, Andretti, and others. "

— *Jack Arute*

" At NASCAR's first Brickyard 400, with the always upbeat, beautiful, special friend, Linda Vaughn. Linda really created her own niche market, a special ambassador to all of Motorsports. She knows everyone and everyone wanted to know her and call her a friend. A very special, classy lady, our Linda. "

— *Danny Sullivan*

That's my brother Danny Sullivan. I was always proud of him; he always was a true gentleman and racer. This was at the Indianapolis Motor Speedway for the Brickyard 400, not the Indy 500. I about had a heart attack during his spin and win in the 500 in 1985. I never prayed so hard in my life as during that.

He and Mario, both very good friends of mine, were side-by-side in the short chute between Turns 1 and 2 when Danny lost control and spun. I couldn't see through all that smoke and I knew Mario was right there. God just protected them both that day. God was riding with both of them.

A lot of people don't know that Danny ran Formula 1 for a season, in 1983 for the Benetton Tyrrell team and finished in 5th place at Monaco.

With John Paul Jr. at the Speedway. He could drive the wheels off a sports car and won the 24 Hours of Daytona twice, once in 1982 while co-driving with his father John Paul Sr. They also won the 12 Hours of Sebring that year. He came to Indianapolis in the early 1990s, running in the 500 from 1990 to 1994 and did well, but he had a bad accident and broke his foot at Daytona.

Paul Jr. had to follow in his father's footsteps, but Sr. never did run Indianapolis so Jr. had an edge in the family, and I was so proud of him. Anybody who can drive an Indy car and scrape the wall in Turn 4 and still make it is a great driver. And he was a great little brother. There's just such a love affair with this family of mine and John Paul Jr. is a part of it.

Another name linked forever with the Indianapolis Motor Speedway is Jim Nabors, who always sings "Back Home Again in Indiana" before the race. It's a big tradition, one that everyone looks forward to every year. Jim and I have been good friends since 1972 when he first came to the race and I had the official Hurst Oldsmobile pace car. We also did several movies together. He's from Alabama and I'm from Georgia so we're both Southerners. We still stay in touch. In fact, I'm going to Hawaii to see him soon.

Janet Guthrie

Janet Guthrie and I. (Greg Doll Photo)

Janet was the first woman to ever race in the Indy 500. I was first introduced to her by the late, great Mark Donohue, who said to me, "Linda, there's a woman that can run Indy and win. It's Janet Guthrie and she's coming in, I want you to meet her." I was ecstatic to meet her because I'd read about her. She was a great engineer, a brilliant lady. I was so excited to meet her, just from what Mark had said about her.

I found her quite shy and nice, very astute, and I felt an aura between the two of us. I just felt she was going to be able to qualify. She was in a couple of different cars that weren't doing so well and then A. J. asked me what I thought about her. I said, "Why don't you put her in the car and let us both see what we think?" He did and she did damn good. When she passed A. J. on the track, he thought she did a little bit too good!

She was a well-versed lady. I think she took a lot of punishment and abuse from the guys in the pits and inside the garage area because she was a woman and she needed a separate bathroom. I don't think she should have been treated that way and I felt sorry for her a few times along the way. But you know how folks are in the beginning, a little on the redneck side, you know? I stood up for her.

When my mother met her, we were sitting on the pit wall and Janet was wearing sandals. Mother looked down and poked me and said, "Look at that, she's got on toe rings. I've never seen toe rings before."

I said, "Mother, so do I." I just had on boots so she couldn't see them. I told Mother, "She might melt those toe rings when she gets in that race car."

I had fun with Janet, on a professional level, and I always talked well about her during my interviews. I was honored and proud, very proud, to represent a woman at Indianapolis. She went on to Pocono, then she drove NASCAR for a bit when Bruton Smith hired her to drive his car, because he knew that she sold tickets. But there again, she wasn't treated as nicely as she should have been, in my view. But all she had to do was put her helmet on and strap in because, honey, she sure could drive.

I see Janet on occasion. Nancy George and I are both glad to have her as a friend. Janet and Lyn St. James certainly made it easier for Danica Patrick to be accepted at Indianapolis. I think Lyn ran 11 Indy 500s, and I got Hurst, Mr. Gasket, and ACCELL to sponsor her.

Janet Guthrie:

"Linda Vaughn was an icon of sex appeal to hundreds of thousands of race fans, especially in NASCAR. But she was also a true lover of the sport, a loving and giving person who contributed a great deal behind the scenes."

It was also the first year that Jim Nabors, who went on to also become a great friend, sang "Back Home Again in Indiana" at pre-race ceremonies, after Tony Hulman asked him to do it that morning.

The entire month of May every year is special because it's all about the grandeur of the Indianapolis 500, but that May in 1972 was probably my best month ever spent at the Speedway. It was a special month.

One thing I do want to clear up here is in regard to A. J.'s book, written by Bill Neely. It had a story about A. J. getting pulled over for speeding while I was riding with him, and he said that I flashed the officer to get A. J. out of the ticket, but that was a bunch of crap and everyone knew it.

A. J.'s wife gave me a copy of his book because she was mad at A. J. for saying something that stupid. I was a little on the hostile side and wanted to whip him for saying something like that, because if I was going to do that I'd do

My baby, Little Al. He's a true friend. Love you always Al Unser! I watched him grow up and I've spent a lot of time with him and Shelley and his kids. His kids are my kids. We're buddies; he's a little brother.

When he was having his difficult times I was there for him. I was there when he won his first race in Milwaukee, and his first win at Indy in 1992. Then he became a two-time winner in 1994. We're like family and I love him dearly. I was especially proud of the Unsers in 1985 when Al Sr. won the CART championship by a point over Junior. (Tom Siefker Photo)

I've known David Letterman for a long time. He used to be a TV weatherman in Indianapolis and I met him when I did the weather report in May. He had June and me on his weather forecast every year. Dave's a character, that's for sure, and I think the world of him. I miss watching him on television, him and Jay Leno both. Letterman and I have stayed friends all these years, as you can tell from this picture.

He did have me on his late-night TV show once, kind of. I was part of his Top Ten List on why you should go to the Indianapolis 500. He went down the list from 10, to 9, 8, and so on. When he got to 2, he showed a picture of me! I told him later, "Well, I was finally on your show but by mention only, but at least you said my name right!" (Tom Siefker Photo)

"It was Garner's first time at the race, Mark's only win at Indy, and Roger's first win at the track."

With Letterman and his team co-owner Bobby Rahal. I think this photo was taken in 2005, when Danica Patrick first raced with them. She just about won it too, leading with only 10 laps to go, but she had to slow to preserve fuel, and finished 4th. Like David, I think the world of Bobby Rahal. He's a great racer, team owner, and a great father. Like father like son, both winners in my book. (Tom Siefker Photo)

Jack Nicholson was the official starter at Indianapolis in 2010 and wore his cherished Los Angeles Lakers hat on the podium to drop the flag. Jack didn't care for too many women but he and I got along well and I like him; I think he's cool. (Tom Siefker Photo)

Mother and my girls in my Sprite suite at the Speedway. Coca Cola was a big sponsor and we used this suite for Hurst; I've had access to it for 30 years. We used it to handle VIPs like James Garner, Hal Needham, Burt Reynolds, Dom Deluise, Jim Nabors, and all the racers and their wives. It was always "the place to be" on race weekend. It was pole position right where you came in from the pits and was a real gathering spot for media, celebrities, drivers and family, and of course my mother was always there. Mrs. Mae loved the Indianapolis 500 and came every year. I'll never forget when they asked driver Fabrizio Barbaza what he liked most about Indianapolis and he said, "Sprite suite!"

This is an oil painting done at IMS by Collin Carter from England. He's done paintings of Mario, A. J., and a lot of the greats. It's a real lovely oil paining of me.

Marco Andretti, my baby. Obviously, I've watched him grow up from a tiny baby to a bad-ass IndyCar driver, and he's one of my children. People have always asked me why I never had any children. I didn't need to, because all the racers' children were my children, and I'm married to racing, honey. (Tom Siefker Photo)

This is my photographer friend Tom Siefker in Indianapolis who has worked with and for me for 35 years.

This photo has nothing to do with racing, but it was taken at the Indianapolis Motor Speedway. This was on the Fourth of July when the Rolling Stones were playing a concert at the Speedway, and that's me with Dr. Greg Chernoff, Nancy George, and Jill Miller on our way to the show. Weren't we hot?

Ashley Judd and I were close when she was married to Dario Franchitti. They're not together any more but she's still a friend. And of course Dario will always be a special friend. (Tom Siefker Photo)

These are two of my dear friends: Tom Siefker, my best guy friend ever who works for me at the Speedway and Cheryl, another photographer and whose husband was a chief mechanic on a team. Bill Simpson made my "fireproof" outfit.

My rookie of the year, Randy Lanier. He drove for Frank Arciero in one of A. J. Foyt's cars in the Indianapolis 500 in 1986. It was a last-minute deal; we got the wonderful Florida Senator Preston Hinn to make a deal with A. J. to buy one of his cars for Randy to race. Randy had long hair so I cut it for him, and I told him, "All you have to do is drive the car. Don't do any of the politicking; I'll do that for you. Just listen to me. You've got a couple of points against you but A. J. believes in you and that's 99 percent of it."

He put the car in the race with the fastest qualifying speed of any rookie, 209 mph, finished 10th, and was Rookie of the Year. Every time I predicted that one of my boys was going to be the Rookie of the Year, I was never wrong, but I never said it until I felt it 100 percent all the way. Randy called me his angel. We had church services next door to my suite and it gave him a place to escape.

This was a great weekend. A. J. with his two boys when they both qualified for the 500. I was real proud of A. J. so I went over to the garage and took this picture with them. Those boys are Foyts, that's for sure. The son and grandson got the seed in them! (Tom Siefker Photo)

Tom Siefker on the right and fellow photographer Michael Easterday on the left. Tom hates the color yellow, especially on his clothes and our outfits were yellow that year. Sorry Tom, you have to wear yellow, it pays the bills! I've worked with Tom for 35 years. He's my confidante, my brother. See that cast on my arm? I broke my wrist right before this race; I got hit by a drunk driver in Daytona in my pace car. (Tom Siefker Photo)

This was during Jim Garner's last visit to Indianapolis. He told me he wasn't feeling well. We called my mother while she was at work, so he got to talk to his sweetheart. He called her up at work because the people at work didn't believe that she was friends with James Garner. So we called her from the starting line at the Indianapolis 500, and then they believed her!

Jim Rathmann on the left, the driver of one of our pace car programs and winner of the Indianapolis 500 in 1960, with John Mecom and me. Jim was great friends with George Hurst and Jack Duffy, and we used to buy our Cadillacs from him. This photo was taken in the John Mecom Suite at the Speedway, which was a traditional meeting place after the race. (Tom Siefker Photo)

I orchestrated this photo of A. J. and Mary Hulman George and Tom Siefker shot it. This photo hangs in Mary's dining room and also in A. J.'s house. Nancy George had bought Mary that shirt. (Tom Siefker Photo)

Danica Patrick and Michael Andretti, in the garage before the start of race. She drove for Andretti Green in 2007, but she had the Argent Mortgage Company sponsorship the year before when she was with Rahal/Letterman, so I think this photo must have been taken in 2006. I was introduced to Danica by Lyn St. James when she was 10 years old. She had braces on her teeth and was the cutest little thing, and she said, "I'm going to run the Indianapolis 500 one day."

I replied, "And I'm going to be standing there with you when you do." Well, boy, she did. That first year, with good equipment and good people . . . the other ladies, like Janet Guthrie and Lyn St. James, set the way, but she could drive, and she came up the hard way. I wish she were still in IndyCars. Had she had a better pit stop she would have won that race. I love her to death. I always give her a Pocket Angel before a race. I tell her, "You can race 'em and kiss 'em." (Tom Siefker Photo)

❝ When I think of Linda Vaughn, I think of a beautiful woman with big blond hair and an even bigger, livelier personality. Linda is such an iconic figure in racing and she's always been such a sweetheart every time I've run into her at the track over the years. One of the things about Linda that has always stuck with me are the coins with angels on them she hands out for good luck before races. I've always thought that was a pretty sweet thing for her to do. ❞

— Danica Patrick

This photo was taken at Indianapolis in 2015, with Jeff Gordon and wife Ingrid and their kids, with Dario Franchitti and Mark Reuss, president of General Motors, and Papa John Schnatter standing next to me.

This is right before Jeff Gordon drove the pace car at the Indy 500 in 2015, after I escorted him down to the starting line. He flew in and had never been in the pace car before. I said, "You can drive anything, just pace it like you want to. You can go into Turn 1 pretty deep too." And he gave me a smile and a nudge. (Tom Siefker Photo)

Every year during the month of May, I do the Bob and Tom radio show in Indianapolis. It's like a tradition for us. This time Nancy George went with me. (Tom Siefker Photo)

Another of my closest friends is Courtney Hansen (right), who is a well-known television personality and spokesperson for a variety of companies. She had never been to the Indianapolis 500 until this year, so Nancy George and I showed her what it was all about. (Tom Siefker Photo)

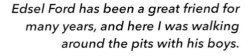

This little boy is an Unser, Al Unser III. We took this photo of the 2nd-place trophy that his dad, Little Al, won at the Phoenix race in 1989 and I made him sign it.

Edsel Ford has been a great friend for many years, and here I was walking around the pits with his boys.

I love this photo of Mario Andretti and me. He's a very close friend to this day, and I visit his winery in Napa Valley every now and then. We're like brother and sister, and I've already mentioned how his kids are my kids, and his grandkids are my grandkids. We're family.

To Linda, Thanks for your support and friendship, I love the sweater. love Arie

and I love the earrings Mieke x

66 I remember reading about Linda and seeing her pictures in magazines and always thought she was quite beautiful; spectacular. So the first time I actually met her I was really shy and kind of taken back and it's really funny I have a picture of us in Milwaukee 1984, you can see me standing next to her and I'm not really looking straight at her.

" Later that same weekend I won my very first race in the United States at the Milwaukee mile and Linda presented me with the trophy and from then on we were friends.

"From those early days of meeting her she has always been great to me and to my wife Mieke and my kids and she's just such an impressive personality. So warm, so kind, so outgoing; really one-of-a-kind. 99

— *Arie Luyendyk*

My Flying Dutch brother Arie Luyendyk and his son Arie Jr. when he won the 500 in 1990 driving for Doug Shierson Racing. That was his first win in the series, driving the red and white Coca Cola/Dominos Pizza car. His average speed in that race was a record that stood for 23 years until Tony Kanaan broke it in 2013.

He was my Rookie of the Year in 1985. In an interview sometime after the race, Arie was asked what the best part about being at the Indianapolis 500 was besides winning, and he said, "Being in the Sprite Suite with Linda." We became great friends are still are today.

Hurst was a big supporter of IROC. The first year, they used Porsche 911s, but then the race cars were all Camaros, and we supplied shifters and parts for them. This was in the winner' circle at Michigan International Speedway with Al Unser and his wife Karen, in 1977. (Photo Courtesy Motor Racing Research Center's National Speed Sport News Collection)

This is the true matriarch of the Indianapolis Motor Speedway, Mary Hulman. I always made it a point to speak with Mary before she said the iconic "Gentlemen, start your engines." She began that tradition when her husband, Tony Hulman, who used to give the order, died in 1977, and she also became the Chairman of both the Speedway and the family business Hulman & Co. Her last time giving the command was in 1996, and I think that's when this photo was taken. She died at the age of 93, two years later.

Justin Wilson the morning of the Indianapolis 500 two years ago, on the Bob and Tom show on Q95 in Indianapolis. Justin and I were teasing each other about our accents. What a lovely guy. We lost him tragically in 2015 when he was hit by debris during a caution period. (Tom Siefker Photo)

At the Indianapolis 500, at the start of one of our parade laps. Sitting on the pit wall in the background, with the blue shirt, just over my shoulder, is Jack Duffy, public relations man extraordinaire!

"I had a little bit of a crush on Rick, as you can tell in this photo."

Rick Mears made it look like he was on rails at the Indianapolis Motor Speedway. When he first showed up on the scene, Mother really took to him. I had a little bit of a crush on Rick, as you can tell in this photo. (Hugh Baird Photo)

Dennis Firestone came from road racing and drove the Gurney Eagle IndyCar for John Buttera and Ronnie Capps. He is not a part of the Firestone family so he didn't come to Indy because he had a golden spoon in his mouth. He came to Indianapolis because he had a golden foot. He was a very accomplished road racer and sports car racer, and I'm quite honored and pleased that he did well in IndyCars.

This was taken at the Michigan race, and he ended up flying back home to California with Mother and me. When we got on the airplane we still had champagne all over us from Victory Circle. We put him in the middle seat between Mother and me and we all had such a good time on the way back home. (Hugh Baird Photo)

This is Debbie Poulson of C&R Racing, Nancy George, myself, Alice Hanks (wife of Sam Hanks who won the Indianapolis 500 in 1957), the lovely Courtney Hansen, and Allegra East (Nancy and my friend who worked in public relations). (Tom Siefker Photo)

My friend and photographer Tom Siefker had this painting done of Mario Andretti, and I presented it to Mario at a fundraiser with Debbie Snider and Nancy George. (Tom Siefker Photo)

"Every time we get to catch up is a treat; our conversations have ranged from the delightfully inappropriate to the sad as we remember lost friends."

I love this picture with Dario Franchitti, the best, most precious man. He missed his first Indy 500 last year because of his accident, but he's a papa now. He told me at Sonoma that he was going to be, and then later on showed me pictures. I love him, very dear to me, and he won the Jim Clark Memorial Award that I was so proud to present to him. (Tom Siefker Photo)

" Linda Vaughn, the ageless force of nature that is my friend. This picture was taken at last year's 500. Since I retired we had more time to enjoy the madness and wonder that is the pre race at Indianapolis together. When going anywhere with Linda it's always hilarious to see men of all ages lose their cool as they catch sight of her then build up the courage to come up, have a chat, and ask for a selfie. She is always so gracious. All my Scottish friends who come to the 500 every year have crushes on Linda!

"I first met Linda in the green room before the 500 parade (I believe in 2002). Luckily, she came up and said hello; just as well as I was too shy to say hello! I was in awe.

"Every time we get to catch up is a treat; our conversations have ranged from the delightfully inappropriate to the sad as we remember lost friends.

"In my memorabilia collection I have my 10 Indianapolis 500 starters rings; they come in a wooden box with the race logo etched into it. Inside each of those boxes is the ring and a small Pocket Angel that Linda gave me every year before the race for safety. I treasure those rings, but equally I treasure the gifts from my friend. "

— Dario Franchitti

Sir David Hobbes. I watched him race Formula 1 in England and all over the world, plus some 24-hour races here. I also had the opportunity to watch his last Formula 1 race. Sir David is quite the entertainer and a dear friend. The young lady in this photo is with the Chamber of Commerce in Talladega.

I presented Little Al with an oil painting of him that was commissioned at the Performance Racing Industry show in Indianapolis. He gave it to his mother. (Tom Siefker Photo)

" I've known Linda since I was a little boy, going to races with my dad. She's wonderful to see at the racetrack, she's been there forever, and I just love her to pieces. She's the First Lady of auto racing and she's an absolute icon and staple of IndyCar racing."

— Al Unser, Jr.

Playboy and make a *lot* of money. I would *never* do anything like that. That book was incorrect; Bill Neely made a huge mistake and A. J. didn't proofread it before it went to print, and everybody at the Speedway was mad at A. J. for saying that about me. It was BS; he was just teasing the cop and that's all there was to it.

Other good memories of the Indianapolis 500 that stick out are when Little Al won, when Arie Luyendyk won, and especially when Mario Andretti won in Andy Granatelli's car and we all went to the STP party afterward. During practice for the race, Mario had a wreck and burned his nose, but then he won the race and it was just awesome. When A. J. Foyt, Al Unser Sr., and Rick Mears each won their fourth races; that was really special.

Those memories are near and dear to me, but they've all been so special to me that to pick just one is hard. That's like trying to pick my favorite car. I can't just choose one! Since my first time there in 1963, I haven't missed a single Indianapolis 500, and as long as I'm still alive I never will miss that race.

Geoff Brabham is the offspring of great Sir Jack Brabham, probably one of the finest car builders in the world. The second year they came to the Indianapolis Motor Speedway, with Jim Clark, they had just won the Formula 1 world championship. Sir Jack was a great entrepreneur and car builder, and his son Geoff followed suit.

He was a chip off the old block. Geoff did quite well and is a lovely person. He's from Australia and used to tease me about "What's down under? It's what's down under that counts."

I would say, "Your feet." He was a lead foot and he did really well at Indianapolis, and I'm proud to know the whole Brabham family, especially his lovely handsome wonderful father who we just lost this year. (Hugh Baird Photo)

" Even before I came to the United States to race in the late 1970s, I had heard about Linda from my dad; his eyes always lit up when he mentioned her! When our paths finally crossed (and this photo could have been that time) I was struck by what a truly nice person she was who absolutely had time for everyone. Her unbelievable talent in remembering names always amazed me. Linda has been a true shinning light in our sport for decades. "

— Geoff Brabham

7

FORMULA 1, SPORTS CARS AND MORE RACING

As Miss Hurst Golden Shifter, I obviously spent a lot of time in Indianapolis every May because the Indy 500 takes up the entire month of May. Between that and all the NASCAR and NHRA/AHRA/IHRA drag races we did, there were even more races that were thrown into the mix, and I loved them all.

James Garner in the Grabber Oldsmobile 442 at the start of the Baja 1000, the year we won our class. What a man, and that's all I have to say!

Danny Ongais and I at the start of the Baja 1000 in Ensenada, Mexico, by Mickey Thompson's race truck. Weren't we a cute couple?

Through my experiences at Indianapolis, I had gotten to know some of the Formula 1 drivers that came to race the 500, like Graham Hill, Jimmy Clark, and of course Mario Andretti. That opened up an entire world of racing that I had never experienced before: Formula 1.

My close friendship with Mario is what took me to Europe to see my first Formula 1 race, the Grand Prix of Monaco. We stayed in a hotel in Monaco and I could hear and feel the sounds of those Ferrari engines screaming through the narrow streets of the Monaco circuit. It was really something! I love the sounds of the thundering American V-8s of NASCAR and the drag races, and the screaming Offys and turbocharged monsters at Indianapolis, but the Formula 1 engines made an entirely different kind of music altogether. It was intoxicating. I wasn't a fixture on the Formula 1 scene like I was in the other motorsports, but it was a fun chapter of my life.

Hurst was heavily involved in all types of motorsports and we did them all, from the Baja 1000, to sports car races, Trans-Am, and IROC. There were so many races over all the years that I was Miss Hurst, that even with my excellent memory I'm sure that I'm forgetting some of them. But I can say without reservation that I loved every minute of it.

This was at a Formula 1 race with Mario, and I'm pretty sure that it's the Long Beach (California) Grand Prix in 1977. Today, Long Beach is on the IndyCar/Champ Car schedule, but when it started in 1975, it was a Formula 1 race. In 1977, Mario was driving the gorgeous black and gold John Player Special Lotus and won the race. He won the Formula 1 World Championship the next year, in 1978.

In this photo, Lotus's Jim Endervite is chewing Mario out about something (look at his gesture) and I went to back up Mario. As you can see, I'm looking over seeing if anyone else was going to come bother them, and if so I was going to woop 'em!

Jackie Stewart and I having a conversation at the Long Beach Grand Prix. He was coming to Daytona to do interviews and the telecast and asked for my advice, and I said, "You don't insult the good old boys." It looks like I'm reprimanding him here, but I'm not.

He and I were very serious with each other and always had a great admiration for each other. I loved working with him and I loved watching him drive. That Tyrrell Formula 1 car really blew me away with those six wheels. I watched him quite closely and he was a devout friend of Jimmy Clark's so we were wonderful friends. He and his wife are still my friends.

From Formula 1 to the Baja 1000: talk about different worlds! We sponsored the Baja 1000 so I went every year. The year this photo was taken, Danny Ongais (right) was driving the truck with Mickey Thompson (left); he got lost and broke down. I was worried sick about him out in the middle of nowhere, but he finally got back to the hotel where we were all staying.

This was at end of the race in Baja when Garner won and I presented him the trophy. I think the couple on the right in this photo owned the restaurant or hotel where we were staying. Weren't we quite the couple?!

Here I am at another IROC race in the 1970s. I'm pretty sure this is at Riverside. My God, I was skinny! I was a vegetarian back then, but it only lasted about three years because my muscle mass got all terrible. (Photo Courtesy Bill Daniels)

" I have wonderful and warm memories of the First Lady of Motorsports, my longtime friend, Linda Vaughn, shown here with George and me. Linda and I met at Daytona when she was Miss Firebird and our friendship, which I cherish greatly, has continued to this day, long after she ceased to be Miss Hurst Golden Shifter.

Obviously Linda has a great personality and is the ultimate 'people person,' who over her long career, got along with everyone, including all the race drivers' and the car owners' wives and girlfriends. She has a tremendous propensity to remember names and make all those she meets feel very special and important.

"It didn't matter what event she appeared at, whether it was a NASCAR, NHRA, USAC, or CART race or function, she stood out above every other personality. Besides, you would have to be blind not to notice her considerable frontal attributes!

"I am honored to call her my friend. "

— Parnelli Jones

Here I am between George Follmer and Parnelli Jones at a Trans-Am race, I think the one in St. Jovite, Canada. I loved Trans-Am. We had Hurst shifters in all the Trans-Am cars and it was a fabulous series. They should recreate it now. My golly I'd like to go back to that. And what a skill; what a different touch to their driving it took. I really enjoyed it. I know both George and Parnelli very well and see them at the Motorsports Hall of Fame ceremony every year.

George is in good health and Parnelli is still built like a brick you-know-what (he really stays in shape). George went out with all of my Hurstettes because he was single and they were all good looking.

Parnelli drove our car, the Hurst Agajanian Special, at Indianapolis, and I watched his kids grow up. Ray Brock and his family would have big parties and we'd all be there. We still stay in touch and we've stayed family all these years.

That's a great driver, that Rufus (Parnelli's real name is Rufus Parnell Jones). He could really drive a car on dirt, and Lord have mercy! He'd kick dirt all over A. J., then A. J. would get mad at him and Mario would come through there and here comes Big Al and whip 'em all and not say a word. It was so much fun!

" The Hut Hundred was one of the highlights of my USAC career, made even more incredible when A. J. and Linda joined me in Victory Circle.

— Jeff Gordon

Denny Hulme and I are talking strategy at a Can-Am race. Denny was also a Formula 1 World Champion, in 1967, and went on to drive the hell out of those McLarens in the Can-Am series, where he won the championship five times in a row (from 1967 to 1971). He got the nickname "The Bear" because he could be gruff and he was a big guy, but he was a very sweet and lovely friend. He was from New Zealand and we just loved each other's accents.

This is during practice at the 24 Hours of Daytona, and that's Billy Krauss in Mickey Thompson's Corvette. Junior Johnson also drove the car for a bit in this race, and qualified it on the pole, but then handed over the driving duties to Billy. He finished 3rd in the race, behind Paul Goldsmith's Pontiac and A. J. Foyt's Corvette.

Pete Brock was known for the Brock Racing Enterprises (BRE) Datsuns that he built and raced in SCCA sports car events in the 1960s and 1970s. But before that he helped Carroll Shelby develop and build the greatest Cobra in the world, the Daytona Cobra Coupe. He lived next door to Joe Schubeck in Henderson, Nevada, and I'd gone to his parties every Halloween during the SEMA show. Pete is very interesting, a cute thing, and also a great writer, a great entrepreneur, and he did brilliant things with Carroll Shelby. My hat is off to him, and I have great respect for him.

❝ There's no forgetting Linda Vaughn! Probably one of the most spectacular looking women in racing . . . ever. The real surprise was in getting to know her. Linda had more insight on both the sport and business of racing than anyone I ever met in the game. Her inside knowledge of who really had the skill and backing to make it in the big time was phenomenal.

"Linda could have been a top team manager, a ruling sanctioning body exec, or perhaps a top racing TV commentator. Her intelligence and ability to see short term how a race was developing or long term where the sport was headed would have made her commentaries the most interesting part of any broadcast, but I suppose her business acumen kept her where she thought she could do best.

"I love Linda. She's never changed; the impossibly smart, beautiful Georgia country girl we all dreamed about having as the girl next door. Best of all she's been a great and loyal friend. ❞

— Peter Brock

8 | TV, MOVIES AND CELEBRITIES

My first real brush with "celebrity" or fame when it came to a nationwide audience was when I won the Miss Poultry Princess contest in Dalton, Georgia. That led me to a trip to Las Vegas and a screen test, which ended up being for the television show Hawaiian Eye with Robert Conrad. I ended up getting a part in the show, and that was a big deal for a little country girl from Dalton!

We did a television special with John Denver, and that's me with Al Unser Sr. and Roger Penske at Riverside. You can see the sound-man back there doing a sound check.

After that, my duties with Hurst racing, going to all the races, the Armed Forces shows, and everything that those entailed, pretty much took up all of my time, so I didn't do very much more TV until I got a call from Kathleen Giampetroni. Her husband was Angelo Giampetroni, the owner of Gratiot Auto Parts in Detroit, a big customer of all the Hurst brands. Because she was there from the beginning, I'll let her tell the story behind my fantastic relationship with Gratiot and the Detroit automotive scene.

When I won the Miss Poultry Princess contest in Georgia, part of the prize was a screen test for the TV show Hawaiian Eye *with Bob Conrad. That's my beautiful friend Virginia on the far left, who came with me from Dalton, Georgia (where she still lives) as my chaperone. Look how sweet I look, with the skirt my mother made for me, and my little white blouse and pearls.*

Here we are prepping for the screen test. Bob Conrad was such a nice man, and he even came to my party in Los Angeles with roses the night they crowned me Miss Hurst Golden Shifter. I was so proud that a famous movie star came to my crowning! I was so excited. That whole time was such an experience.

Kathleen Giampetroni

❝ Angelo decided to do billboards with Linda, and the most famous one was on I-75 near 8 Mile. It was Alan's idea to take the Gratiot Auto Supply billboard and make her a cutout figure above and below it, like she was standing next to it. Everybody just loved that billboard. ❞

— Kathleen Giampetroni

❚❚ My husband Angelo had been in business for a long time before I met him, with a huge mail order and wholesale business. George Hurst had come to Angelo's store one day and asked Angelo what he thought of the product and whether or not he wanted to order any of it. That started their relationship. So Angelo knew George Hurst years before he knew Linda.

"Once George hired Linda, she would go to the SEMA show, and that's when we met, just casually. She would come to the [Detroit] Cobo Hall car show and Angelo

This was a billboard that Gratiot did with my picture. Angelo sure knew how to advertise his business! There was this one, and then another one that had my whole body standing next to the sign. Some guy stole my legs off of the billboard and brought them to the Autorama for me to sign. I told him, "Why don't you go back and steal the rest of me?" I think he did! (Photo Courtesy Gratiot Auto Supply)

would pick her up at the airport, but this was before I was involved with the business. He only had one retail store in the beginning, but they shipped all over the world: Germany, Australia, Mexico, you name it. I didn't know anything about cars when I met him and I didn't start working with him until our kids were in about the fourth or fifth grade.

Kathleen Giampetroni *CONTINUED*

"One day he came home from work and told me that two crazy guys came into his office and wanted him to do some radio jingles and stuff like that. I told him I wanted to talk to them so we did, and I was just crazy about both of them. They were both young ad guys and one of them, especially, was full of energy and ideas, and I clicked with them right away. So we started doing a few radio jingles.

"Angelo was very creative and was already doing his catalogs by himself. He did everything from laying them out to putting the parts and prices in. He did all that at night when he'd come home. We did a few radio ads and they were very successful immediately, and we saw a big increase in business. Then one of the guys suggested we do some 15- to 30-second television spots. I thought they were crazy but they said that it was really cheap if we went on the right stations at the right time, so we started looking into it.

"During conversations about what they wanted to do with the commercials, I said, 'Why don't you use somebody like Linda Vaughn and just pretend she's walking through the pits like she does, talking to the guys. Her whole spiel she has while walking through the pits; she could just say that on TV.'

"We weren't more than casual acquaintances at that time, but I had watched her in the business and thought she was very talented as far as knowing the business. They thought I was crazy, but they agreed to try it. They flew her in and Alan immediately saw what her personality was. Angelo saw that she could do this kind of thing and he instantly turned into Fellini. He thought he was running a movie set!

"He said, 'I want her to wear the go-go boots like she does at the races, and the white shorts and a Gratiot T-shirt.' And he made sure that the T-shirt was really tight, and they put clothespins on the back so it said Gratiot Auto Supply across her chest really well on TV.

"It was a lot of laughs, and it was all by the seat of our pants, but Angelo always knew what he wanted; he was an artistic type that way. He always designed all the stores and displays, and our stores were always beautiful and way ahead of their time.

"So he laid out parts all over the floor and hung some parts up high and she just walked through and said, 'Do you love your car, truck, or van, man? Then come down to Gratiot Auto Supply and tell 'em Linda sent you.' And we made sure we put her name across the bottom of the screen so it would go across like a ribbon, the way they do on the news networks now, that said 'Linda Vaughn, Miss Hurst Shifter.'

"We must have started doing the commercials around September and they were really popular, but then Channels 7 and 4 wrote us letters trying to take her off the TV because it was 'too sexy.' I called our lawyer immediately and told him to write them a nasty letter, because at the same time, there was a health club in Detroit that had commercials on TV with four girls running down the beach in bikinis with their boobs bouncing all over the place.

"I told our lawyer, 'You write them a letter and tell them that if they want to take ours off because it's too sexy, they'd better take that one off too or they're going to see us in court!' They immediately changed their minds, because when they started those shenanigans we were on prime time, like during the 6 and 11 o'clock news with 30-second ads. All of a sudden we had a lot of men coming into the stores in suits, during the day, and of course they didn't know one damn thing about high-performance parts, but they were saying, 'Where's Linda?'

"A few months after the commercials started airing, the Cobo Hall Show came around. So I picked Linda up at the airport and told her, 'Get ready girl, you're a star. Everybody in Detroit is talking about you.'

"She didn't believe me until we were walking through the airport and there was a guy there waxing or cleaning the floors in the airport, and he turned around and said, 'Are you the girl on TV?'

"When we got to Cobo Hall, it was packed and people kept trying to rush her and get her autograph, so we had to put stanchions around our display. We didn't realize that people would be coming down to just grab at her, so the second night we got some big security guards in place.

"By that time, we had about six stores (we ended up with 8 at one point), and Angelo made some cutouts (this was way before cutouts were even heard of) of her and had them standing in the stores, looking just like she did on TV. It was a great couple of years, but then President Carter got into office and caused so many problems with everybody's businesses, and we had the OPEC oil embargo and all of a sudden gas prices were just over the top. Everybody was hurting, and the shadetree mechanics put their cars away; they weren't going out to the racetrack or doing anything.

"Around 1980 it all hit the fan and all of a sudden our stores were like ghost towns. We went out of business about that time. It was a brief period, but it was a lot of fun."

This is Kathleen Giampetroni and me on Easter Sunday at her and Angelo's house in Bloomfield Hills, Michigan. Since I loved to cook, I cooked everything in her freezer: ham, turkey, a roast, potatoes. She wasn't feeling well, but I made her go outside and take this photo with me. I found this hat; that's their beautiful house on the lake in the background, where I used to do all her commercials for Gratiot Auto Supply. (Photo Courtesy Gratiot Auto Supply)

Angelo Giampetroni and I in my hot rod Lincoln at the St. Ignace (Michigan) show; we call Angelo Cecil B. DeMille. He had the first warehouse to put the money into TV ads, and he had 14 Gratiot Auto Supply stores. I owe a lot to Angelo and his wife Kathleen.

When she told me that I was "going to be a star," I didn't know what she was talking about, but when we got to the Autorama at Cobo Hall; my word, I got mobbed! I had the husbands, sons, grandkids, and all there because they had seen those Gratiot TV ads.

We worked so well together and Angelo's ads were also great for Hurst. We sold a lot of shifters through Gratiot. I'd do their warehouse shows, go to each warehouse store opening, and we did about half a dozen commercials over the years. I still have people yell "Gratiot Auto Supply" when I'm in a parade there.

I tell George Barris, "Georgie Porgie puddin' and pie, kiss the girls and make 'em cry." But he never made me cry. George was friends with George Hurst for years and I met him and Isky the same day in 1966. We've been friends ever since, though sadly he just passed away recently. (Photo Courtesy SEMA)

This was such a fun experience, making Stroker Ace with Burt Reynolds and Hal Needham. I knew Hal from the races and had met Burt several times, but we didn't get to really know each other until this movie. Bill Neely and Bob Ottum wrote the book Stroker Ace and wanted me to play myself in the film, so they called and hired me. I became a member of AFTRA and SAG with that job, and got paid more money this time.

Mother made this costume; I think I was a size 1. The costume guy loved me because I made all my own costumes, or Mother did. (Photo Courtesy Will Cronkite)

That sign says Daytona but we were actually in Atlanta. We had all the drivers there. Tim Richmond was a real character that whole time. Jim Nabors was there, and we all had a lot of fun on-set. It was hilarious. Burt and I get along famously; as you can see, we're cracking up here.

Hal was mad and came down off his lift yelling, "That's not in the script!" and Burt is defending me. But I never got a script, I was just being myself.

I had to tell Burt, "Well, you left me at Talladega" and he said, "What for?" I said, "You told me you went to get a loaf of bread." They left that scene in but they took a lot of it out, which is too bad because we had a lot of funny stuff.

I did my own hair and Loni Anderson was upset because mine looked better than hers. I went to the dressing room and she asked me who did my hair, so I said, "Get in here, sit down, and be still." And I did her hair. I had Aquanet that holds in the humidity.

This was Dottie Parker, Lorne Greene from Bonanza, me, and Booper at the airport hotel we all stayed at for the Atlanta 500. Lorne had a special appearance at the track, I think he was the Grand Marshal that year, and this was us getting ready to go out to the track the morning of the race. He was so sweet, and liked us girls.

Actor Jim Caviezel (he played Jesus in The Passion of the Christ) is a lovely man, probably one of the quietest, shyest men I've ever met. He was our guest at Indianapolis and is a good friend of Tony George. (Tom Siefker Photo)

God bless Brock Yates. This shot of us was taken when he came up to do an interview with me at Bakersfield.

Brock and I started on the story and worked our way through the pits, when we were told that Garlits got hurt at Lions, when he lost his foot in a horrible clutch explosion. So Brock and I jumped on a plane and went down to the LA airport and were there when Pat Garlits walked off the plane. I looked her right in the eyes and never blinked.

She told me later, "I knew, Linda, if you closed your eyes, I had lost Don."

I said, "No, we haven't lost him." And then we went to the hospital.

Brock and I were working on a book but he's come down with Alzheimers now. He is still alive in body, but his spirit is gone. It's too bad because it was going to be one hell of a book. "We'll take that one to heaven with us, Brock."

Troy Polamalu from the Pittsburgh Steelers is a race fan, and came to Indianapolis a few years ago. This was down on the track before the race.

Little Al Unser was being honored at a function at the Biltmore in Los Angeles and Mikhail Baryshnikov performed there, then we went backstage and met him. This is him between me and one of Al and Shelley Unser's friends. He came for drinks with us later and tried to come home with me but no, no, no, no. I like his dancing but that's as far as it goes! (Tom Siefker Photo)

This is Rob Van Winkle, aka Vanilla Ice, at Barrett-Jackson a few years ago. I just love him. He's sweet, which you can tell by what he's done for the kids' charity at Barrett-Jackson.

Country superstar Reba McEntire's son Shelby Blackstock was racing in the Nationwide 300 at Indianapolis and we met in Nancy George's suite in the Pagoda. We wanted to meet each other because we're both Southerners, and this photo shows us having a good ol' Southern talk. Reba's quite an actress and a lovely singer of course, but she's also a true race fan. She's definitely hooked on racing.

PGA golfer Fuzzy Zoeller has his own vodka with these exquisite bottles. He is a great personality to work with, and he sponsors Ed Carpenter's Indy race team. I have one of these collector's bottles in my kitchen and it's still full. (Photo Courtesy Tom Siefker)

What a great group. It was a real treasure for me to get to know the Rolling Stones. We had a great time. Enough said! I met the Stones through my old friend Bobby Keys who played saxapone with them. They were also good friends with Al Unser Jr. and Chip Ganassi. They liked racing and I loved the Stones. They presented me with an all-access hard card to go to all their concerts during the Voodoo Tour. My mother called me once and asked, "Was that you on stage with them ugly boys?" I said, "Yes Mother, but they sure can rock!" One night after a show in Montreal we were all up in their suite having drinks and Ron Wood asked if he could sketch me. He drew a beautiful picture of me; Ron Wood is quite the artist.

9 AWARDS AND HALLS OF FAME

When it was created in the 1960s, SEMA was called the Speed Equipment Manufacturers Association. It has since been renamed the Specialty Equipment Market Association. Whatever it is called, SEMA is the heart of the whole hot rodding and racing community.

This is when I got the SEMA Hall of Fame award, thanks to the efforts of the wonderful Dick Wells. What an honor it has been, and still is, that I work with SEMA so closely. If they ever call and need me, I'll go.

Of course working with Robert E. Petersen was one of the highlights of my life. That man was brilliant. I stay in tune with his spirit when I visit Joe Schubeck and Gigi Carlton (who was Mr. Petersen's longtime assistant) because I feel as if I'm walking back into his presence.

It's the trade organization that all of the companies, including Hurst, belong to and we meet every year in November in Las Vegas for the SEMA Show. I've been going ever since I became Miss Hurst Golden Shifter in 1966, and it's like coming home for a big family gathering every year. I love SEMA and all the companies involved in it, and I was very honored to be inducted into the SEMA Hall of Fame in 1985.

SEMA Hall Of Fame
SEMA SHOW 2013

What an impressive group this is, the members of the SEMA Hall of Fame in 2013. Next to me is my Georgie, George Barris. Also in this esteemed crowd are Jimmy Kerr, Ray Lipper, Bob Airheart, Leo Kagan, Ed and Bobby Spar, Angelo Giampetroni, Rich Rawlings, Herb Fishel, Don Smith, Vic Edlebrock Jr., and so many more distinguished people. I'm very honored to be one of the few women in the Hall of Fame at SEMA, made even better because it is voted on by your peers.

The International Motorsports Hall of Fame is in Talladega (IMHoF), Alabama. Its official saying is, "The men and women enshrined in this facility are not only the best of the best in motorsports, they are an important part of our world." I couldn't agree more, and I try to visit every year. I'm so proud to be a big part of the IMHoF.

Carroll Shelby was supposed to speak at the IMHoF, but he was late getting there so I stood in for him. You can see by the smile on my face that I was really terrorizing everybody.

Look at all these good-looking men! This was in Washington, D.C., when we went to the White House representing SEMA. From left to right are Brock Yates, Sal Fish, Snake, Billy Gibbons, and Elton Alderman from Prolong. When they introduced me to everyone, I said, "How many of you senators had a Hurst shifter?" You should have seen all the hands. We were presented awards from our government for what SEMA brought to the world of American-made parts, and I was so honored to be with this group.

Marla Moore (left) and Tammy Holland from Competition Cams (right) from Hypertech are both very heavily involved in SEMA, and I just love those girls. Here they recognized my hard work with the organization, and they deserve to be recognized as well. They're wonderful ladies I'm real proud to be part of this family.

Kathleen Giampetroni found this jacket in New York City and gave it to me for SEMA.

This was at the Hall of Fame luncheon, when Joe Hurdka (left) and Don Prudhomme (right) were my guests. That was the same year that my mother died. She became quite ill and then I lost her and became ill myself. I went through a lot that year; you can tell because I was so thin. Snake and Joe both loved my mother, and she loved them too. She used to tell Snake, "Hey Snake, snakes crawl at night."

She especially loved Joe Hrudka for giving me an opportunity when I was going through my divorce in 1987, which was a bad time in my life. It was very bad on me but the industry was there for me. I faced a lot of bridges and crossed them.

Joe had been trying to get me to go to work for him at Mr. Gasket for years, but I said I'd never turn my back on George Hurst. Then one night, Joe and Carroll Shelby called me and Shelby said, "Okay Linder, we're going to buy Hurst. What's your excuse now?"

So we had a meeting and I gave Joe my contract. He said, "I've never paid anyone that much before," so I told him to look at the bottom of the contact and what it gave back in return: I had a direct connection to the OEM and could bring him OEM sales and that made him lots of money.

Thank heaven for Joe Hrudka, because had it not been for him, I would have lost my house. I went to the hospital thinking I had cancer, but the only cancer was the stress of going through that divorce. When the doctor cleared me of having cancer, Joe gave me a job and I opened all the major warehouses for him, and I needed the salary because I had to show the bank that I had a job and salary and could therefore save my home.

I took my attorney Sam "Hot Rod Lawman" Eidy with me to the Hall of Fame luncheon this time. This is George Barris and Corky Coker stopping by our table to say hello. This is when we talked about getting George into the Hall of Fame.

This was working the SEMA Show. Look at that Dolly Parton hairdo and outfit! What I like about this picture is the wives. The wives come to get pictures for their husband's Christmas presents and bring their daughters and grandkids; it's a real family affair.

When I first came to SEMA, I knew I wanted to clean it up because they used to have girls that were practically nude and rude. I said, "No, if we're going to have the ladies come to our SEMA Show, we have to clean up this act right now."

I like to be sexy, but I'm a lady and I want to be treated like one. A few of us got together and put together a SEMA luncheon for the ladies, and I was one of the guest speakers that first year. It grew and grew and I'm really proud to be a part of that, to tell the women that we appreciate them being behind their husbands, businesses, and the industry, and this photo is a perfect example of that.

This was a very special night at the IMHoF in Talladega. Behind me are all the members of the Hall and I'm standing with the Hall's Don Naman (left) and Larry Camp from NASCAR. That's Carroll Shelby in the red bow-tie over Larry's shoulder.

Also at the Hall of Fame banquet, this is me with Neil Bonnet (right) and Mel Larson. Mel brought NASCAR to Las Vegas; he worked at Circus Circus and helped build the Las Vegas Motor Speedway with his partners. This was the night that Neil was inducted into the IMHoF.

We were at Daytona on Valentine's Day every year so he always brought me flowers. His wife said that I'm the only other sweetheart that he can have. What a shame when we lost him; he was such a handsome and wonderful man, and a great driver. He had never done any drag racing but was going to do some announcing at the NHRA Winternationals, so I helped him with it and we hit it off really well. He was very special to me and we all miss him.

At the IMHoF luncheon with Bill and Marion Brakefield, their grandbaby, me, and Sandy Jackson (the Registered Nurse at Indianapolis). Nancy George got me that beautiful knit dress.

At the IMHoF banquet in 2005 in the lovely white Bob Mackie gown. Those shoes and purse cost more than the gown!

This was a lot of trouble right here! This is my friend Trudi Stalker, Tony Stewart, me, Ronnie Capps, Nancy George, and John Force. In 2012, they gave me a roast at the Lucas Family Sports Castle in Indianapolis and it was quite a night! Darrell Gwynn dressed as me, and there were very heartfelt things said from Chip Ganassi, Lyn St. James, Tony Stewart, John Force, and so many more. When it was done we continued the party at the hotel until 6:00am. They didn't feel very good the next morning! (Samantha Siefker Photo)

Michael Knight is the President of the American Auto Writers Racers and Broadcasters Association, and this is him presenting me an honorary Jim Chapman Award for excellence in motorsports public relations in Indianapolis.

The Chapman Award is highly coveted by many in the industry as the highest honor in racing public relations. It is named in memory of Chapman, the legendary PR executive and innovator, who worked with Babe Ruth, Dan Gurney, Bobby Unser, Mario Andretti, Bill France Sr., and Avis Rent-a-Car founder Warren Avis among many others. He also brought PPG into the sport and made a lot of money for everyone.

Chapman, named IndyCar racing's "most influential man" of the 1980s, died in 1996 at age 80. He was a sweet southern gentleman and always dressed fabulously, and I'm honored to carry on his name and award. As you can see in the photo, I was crying, very humbled to have received it.

I'm very close to the entire Barrett-Jackson auction family. I've sold two of my Hurst Oldsmobiles at Barrett-Jackson. The first one went to a man in Pennsylvania when I was really sick and had to pay hospital bills, and this 1979 one sold in Florida.

The buyer was Craig Jackson himself. His wife, Carolyn, and daughter used to have a 1979 Oldsmobile and Carolyn told Craig, "Buy that for me, sweetheart" so he did.

We put my Hurst Oldsmobile into their T-Gen Foundation in the names of his father and brother, both of whom died of prostate cancer. My car made $740,000 for the foundation to help find a cure for prostate cancer. The last gentleman to buy it was John Stuluppi, when Sharon Stone and I sold it on-stage at Barrett-Jackson. My nephew Gerald Vaughn has one just like it.

This was at another of the SEMA Hall of Fame luncheons. Look at all these movers and shakers of the automotive industry. Bob Airheart, Tom Shedden from Cragar, Speedy Bill Smith, George Elliott, Vic Edelbrock, Wally Parks (whose arm I'm holding), Carroll Shelby, Joe Hrudka, Dick Wells, Lou Senter, Alex Xydias, and more. And I'm the only woman there. What an honor.

I won the Bob Russo Award at the IMHoF. Bob Russo was one of the best press men to ever come down the pike. He was the public relations director for Riverside International Raceway and used to give me the hardest time. The first time he met me he said, "What makes you think I should give you a pit pass?"

I said, "Thirteen sponsorships that we ran through your racetrack, that's what I think!"

To win this coveted award in his name was a real honor.

This was right before my last Hall of Fame lunch together with Speedy Bill and Shelby. They were terrorizing me that day, like two big brothers and their demon sister.

Bill would say, "You're not married yet? When are you going to get married and settle down?"

And Shelby told Bill, "Hell I'd a married Linda, but she'd a killed me."

Right there is pure love, folks. My boyfriend Greg is a gems dealer and he gave me that emerald necklace. My mother said, "That sure is beautiful, but what is it?" and I said, "My next house." It was the most gorgeous Christmas present anyone has ever given me. Shelby loved that necklace.

Another photo from the Hall of Fame, with Joe Amato, Shav Glick, George Bignotti, Bobby Unser, Danny Ongais, Geoff Brabham, Bill Simpson, Bobby Rahal, and George Follmer. This was the night I received the Bob Russo Award.

" Unique. That's an adjective that describes Linda Vaughn. Her ability to remember people and their names was amazing: the drivers and their crews, their wives and girlfriends, and the corporate execs. She befriended all of them and was respected and liked by everybody. The fans adored her. Linda has a great talent and was a mainstay of the sport.

"She was and still is a friend to me and all the many people of the racing community. Linda set the standard for Race Queen. Thank you, Linda. "

— George Follmer

Lori Johns

"I think Linda Vaughn is one of the most historically significant icons that ever graced the automotive industry. She has received the accolades and awards for her accomplishments and contributions that are just as integral to the development and history of automotive racing as any other promotional role. No one made Linda Vaughn, she made herself!

"She became my friend and ally from the moment that I stepped into racing and she got to know me. Linda is an astute judge of character. She is one of the most intelligent people that I have ever met. She tried to help me in so many ways by teaching me how to pose for pictures and attempted to teach me her technique for remembering the name of everyone she ever met (unfortunately, I wasn't sharp enough).

"She remains one of the most well-connected people alive in this industry. Linda knew everyone and everything that was going on and used that knowledge for the greater good of the sport that she spent her entire life dedicated to promoting. She was the original trophy girl, but she was so much more than that, so much more than most people could ever know or will ever begrudgingly recognize. I have a unique perspective of her, being a woman. She was my friend.

"Most men have a hard time separating women and sex to see past what lies within the power of a beautiful, sexy, and intelligent woman. Even if they see how instrumental a woman who looks like Linda is, was, and can be, they have a very hard time admitting it. It is just too threatening to them. I believe that is why Linda has been left out of a lot of the Legends Events that seem to exclude her. She was there from the beginning and never missed an event for years and years. She deserves so much more from the life she dedicated to our world. She graced it with a sexy, beautiful exterior that has been unmatched by any "trophy girl" on the outside and an unmatched big heart and compelling mind on the inside!

"With one word from her, Linda was able to get sponsors to support me. She had those men's attention and respect because she knew what she was talking about. I cannot believe that after all that she did to try and bring something beautiful to our often hard, greasy, and what could be a very ugly sport, that not one of those people in the industry is willing to take care of her now, after she has given us all that she had."

This is another shot from the IMHoF, with NHRA Top Fuel competitor Lori Johns and 1985 Winston Cup champion Bill Elliott.

" I first met Linda Vaughn while I was running Cup races in the 1980s. No one really ever had to introduce you to Linda; she had such a bubbly personality and she was always the one to approach and introduce herself first.

"My racing career took me many places and it was always wonderful to see Linda, a familiar face, in the garage area and many times in victory lane as my career progressed as well.

"Linda Vaughn is an icon to all racers and will forever be 'Miss Hurst' for generations of us. **"**

— Bill Elliott

Tony Stewart was my date this night at the IMHoF and we presented Red Farmer with the Racing Angel Award. It was a special evening. These two talked me into going to the dirt-track races the next day and my hair was full of Alabama red clay!

This photo was taken at the Nostalgia Drag Racing Association event in York, Pennsylvania, in 2009. In the back row, from left to right are Kenn Schulz, Wally Booth (accepting for Dick Arons), Tom Myl, Jim Lawford, me, Bill Zinkhan, Jimmy King, and "Beaver Bob" McCardle. In the front row are Carl Ruth, Pete Shadinger, Dave Bishop, Bill Drevo Jr., and Marv Ripes.

This was at the Detroit Autorama, before the Ridler's Ball, with Richard and Kyle Petty. We had them come as our special guests, and it was a great night to have them there.

> 66 I don't remember when I first met Linda. She was always at the track, just like my family was. My dad won so many races and she was always in Victory Lane! You can't walk through my dad's house without seeing a picture of her somewhere from some race. She always called herself Aunt Linda to me and my sisters, and in a way she really was. She's family. 99
>
> — Kyle Petty

This is Joe Riley, a big supporter of Barrett-Jackson. He's a Georgia boy and bought my Oldsmobile, so I gave him a Pocket Angel. He bought the car and gave it back to the Foundation for T-Gen research, which does prostate cancer research. He buys and sells a lot of cars at Barrett-Jackson, but he does it because he loves children and does it for the T-Gen foundation.

This is the group that allowed us to raise $700,000 on the sale of my Hurst Oldsmobile for the T-Gen Foundation. To the right of me is Els Chesney, who first bought the car and then gave it back for the Foundation and made Joe Riley (left) buy it. Then they gave it back to me after making all that money for the charity. To the right of Els in the photo is Caroline Jackson and Craig and Shelby Jackson.

In the Barrett-Jackson skybox with George Barris before we sold his Batmobile. From left to right are Shelby Jackson (Craig's daughter and Carroll Shelby's namesake), me, George, Craig Jackson, and Steve Davis. We later sold Batmobile for $6 million and I came out in my Batman outfit.

Snake and I with actors Sharon Stone and Dom DeLouise Jr. at the Barrett-Jackson auction when we sold my 1979 Hurst Oldsmobile.

Darrell Gwynn had a fishing tournament at Daytona before the truck race. Here we are with Mike Skinner and my friend Trudi on pit lane. I've known Darrell Gwynn his whole life. His father Jerry and his mother have always been great friends of mine, and I watched Darrell grow up and win Top Fuel at Seattle driving for Kenny Bernstein. He also won the U.S. Nationals. I call him my little brother, and all his promotions and functions, foundations, if he needs me I always go and help.

Darrell and A. J. Foyt are real close. We call A. J. and say, "Hey fat boy, how ya doin'?" Darrell is so wonderful to continue his livelihood in this sport, and to be in his condition and continue on, people around the world love him and I'm proud to call him my friend.

With SEMA's Peter MacGillivray and our entertainment for the banquet, Sinbad. Peter does a wonderful job for SEMA and I've known Sinbad on and off for 25 years. He is a hoot and every time we see each other we crack up because everyone tries to introduce us all the time.

Willie Nelson is a friend of mine, and when I was on the SEMA entertainment committee they asked if I could get him to play for the SEMA banquet. He was having trouble with the government so SEMA paid him in one-dollar bills in a brown paper sack.

This was the night they put Angelo Giampetroni into the Hot Rod Hall of Fame. In this photo is also Roy Brizio (right), Bobby Alloway, and Peter Toundas, the president of Championship Auto Shows that runs the Detroit Autorama. Pete used to work for Angelo at Gratiot Auto Parts. Angelo and Kathleen hired him as a young boy and we worked together a lot at Gratiot. The way he's accomplished everything is a wonderful example of our industry.

As for the outfit, it was Halloween so I went as Elvira, of course!

There are many other organizations and halls of fame that I'm associated with, including the Performance Racing Industry (PRI) Show and the Barrett-Jackson auction company. Craig Jackson, Steve Davis, and Gary Bennett; those three men I've kind of grown up with all these years, and I knew their fathers. George Hurst took me to my very first Barrett-Jackson auction out in the boonies of the dessert. I wore these really pretty shoes and the damn gravel we had to walk on tore them all to pieces! The whole family has been tremendous to me. I love that whole group, and it's been a 45-year relationship.

Then there is the Die Cast Hall of Fame, the International Motorsports Hall of Fame, NASCAR Hall of Fame. I'm so happy to be associated with all of them, as a member, representative, and just a part of our whole big extended family of racers, businessmen, hot rodders, and enthusiasts.

Some of the highlights of my Hall of Fame events were having George

This was a very special luncheon! I got a phone call from Shelby: "Aw dammit, Linder! You need to come to this luncheon tomorrow!"

I told him I had just gotten in from the road and he said, 'I don't give a damn. You gotta come to the luncheon tomorrow. We're going to celebrate Parnelli; Edsel Ford wants you there, and I want you to sit between me and my wife so we don't fight."

So this is Parnelli Jones, Edsel Ford, me, and Shelby, who was goosing me from behind. This was at the Proud Bird restaurant in Los Angeles.

Mother and I at the Hurst Oldsmobile Club of America Nationals. I was introducing Mother and she had tears in her eyes.

Bob Muravez, aka Floyd Lippencott Jr., on the left with Joe Schubeck and I at the Project 1320 booth at SEMA. Those were steering-wheel earrings and we were going to make them, but the girl behind the project dropped out.

Chip Ganassi presented me with the Living Legends Award at Daytona. He was also my date that evening. I was very proud to have helped Chip get started. We're like brother and sister and have always confided in each other. We're in each other's worlds, and he's a true angel of mine. What a night that was! Mike Helton from NASCAR was there, plus all of the Allisons, and they all said such nice things about me.

Barris, "Georgie," as my date for the SEMA Installation dinner. He showed up in his red Jaguar and I showed up in my red Ferrari Dino, and we were quite the item! I said, "George, will you be my date?" and he met me at the door with a dozen roses.

I was elected into the Die Cast Hall of Fame in Las Vegas with Bruce Meyer (for his work with the Petersen Automotive Museum) and NASCAR champion Rusty Wallace and that was a very special evening. Then there was the Living Legends of NASCAR ceremony during Daytona Speed Weeks, where my date and presenter was Chip Ganassi. Chip's speech was so lovely that I cried. I don't think there was a dry eye in the place.

I appreciate getting all of these Hall of Fame recognitions and I hope I'm going to be around next year to see what's next. I'm not through yet, folks!

10 MY PERSONAL LIFE

If you couldn't tell by now, I'm addicted to racing. It's my drug. I love the cars, the people, the sounds and smells of the cars and the racetracks, and I love competition.

I'm completely "into it" and can never wait until the next round. With ten laps to go in the Indianapolis 500, I'm a nervous wreck. And the first time I went to the Daytona 500, I saw them drafting and thought to myself, "Oh my gosh, I have to go down in the turns and watch Fireball Roberts!" I'm still the exact same way, even after all these years.

It's not just NASCAR, however; it's everything (including IRL, NHRA, IHRA, Off-road racing, Formula 1, and sports car racing) that involves engines, racing, and speed, and that sound that goes along with them. There's no age limit in racing, just like there's no age limit to music. It's absolutely fascinating.

During all the years that I've been in this industry, I have made a lot of incredible friends and unfortunately lost a lot of friends too. But that's not just racing, it's how life works, and while I wish we could have all of them back, that's just the way it goes. None of us get out of here alive; we just hope we cross the finish line under a waving checkered flag!

I never had children. I chose this life instead, but I feel like I do because all the racers' kids are my kids: the Foyts, the Garlits, the Andrettis, the Unsers, the Allisons, and the Pettys! Their kids are my kids, and I honestly feel that way. It has been a complete joy to watch them all grow up and become the fine ladies and gentlemen and the racers that they've become.

Heartfelt Thanks

I owe so much to everyone who helped me get here, but mostly George Hurst and Jack Duffy, who really changed my life. We grew together and built an unbelievable marketing powerhouse with Hurst, Schiefer Clutches, and Hurst Airheart brakes in the early days of the automotive aftermarket, which has grown into an international, multi-billion dollar industry. They were both like my family and I miss them terribly.

❝ Linda has always been so gracious with the fans and so adept at raising money for many charities. She greets everyone by name (I wish I had half her memory for names and faces!), and always makes folks around her feel welcome and special. She may be the most approachable celebrity in racing, and is truly one who has given much more to the sport than gained from it. I'm proud to be her friend, and a fan! ❞

— *Mike Joy*

❝ My dad George has been a drag racer for 40 years so I grew up going to dragstrips all the time. And my dad always had *Hot Rod* magazines, *Super Stock and Drag Illustrated*, and all those, so I obviously knew who Linda Vaughn was but had never met her in person.

"My first national event was the Springnationals in June 1995, when I was 13 years old, and anybody who's been to that race knows that it's either going to be hot as hell or raining. This one was raining, so we ran over to the manufacturers' midway and hung out under the Mr. Gasket tent. My dad nudged me and said, 'Hey, do you know who that is?' And it was Linda Vaughn coming out of the trailer.

"She made her rounds talking to people and eventually came over and started chatting with us. My favorite band is Nirvana and I had on a Nirvana ball cap, and Linda said, 'Oh my gosh I love Nirvana!' Being 13 years old and so into that band, I thought, 'Who is this lady?' So she and I chatted away about music and things for maybe an hour. She didn't have any posters left to sign, so she said, 'Write me a letter and I'll mail you a signed poster.'

"My dad said, 'Everybody into racing needs to have a hug from Linda Vaughn.' At the time I didn't have my growth spurt yet so I was short and came right up to boob level on Linda, and she gave me this great big huge bear hug. My dad said I didn't quit smiling for a week.

"When I got home I went through my dad's magazines looking for anything with Linda in it, then sent a letter to Mr. Gasket trying to get one of those posters. Then I read an interview with her and found out her birthday was on August 14, so I sent her another letter and said, 'You probably don't remember me, blah blah blah,' and sent it to Mr. Gasket again. I had just started high school and was doing homework when the phone rang and my sister answered it. She said, 'There's some lady on the phone for you.' I'm thinking, 'Ohmygod, it's a teacher and I must have screwed up on something.' So I pick the phone up and the first thing she said was, 'Do you still love me?' I'm like, 'Oh my God, it's Linda Vaughn calling me!'

"I don't know what it was; we just hit it off and still talk pretty frequently. At this point, I've known her for 20 years and I see her as a great friend, whereas my dad and his generation are still star struck by her. Not saying I'm not, but I know her more as a friend than anything else. One of the nicest things she's ever said to me, is 'Michael (and only two people in the world call me Michael, my mom and Linda), you are the son that I never had.' To me, that is one of the biggest compliments I've ever had. She's been such an awesome person to know. ❞

— *Mike Krieger*

My beautiful mother and I at a cocktail party, at the AHRA World Finals in Tulsa, Oklahoma, probably in the late 1960s. I miss her every day.

I wanted to make sure to include Doctor Greg Chernoff in this book. He is our plastic surgeon who is the head of our foundation for reconstructive surgery for injured drivers, injured soldiers, and battered women. He's also a magnificent chef, and his mother and I are a lot alike. He calls me his sweet friend. He has magical hands. God bless him. (Tom Siefker Photo)

This is the outfit I wore (above) for one of my first dates with Tim Richmond. "TLR my Superstar" is what I called him. We had a fantastic, very close relationship (below).

I also miss being able to talk to my mother, brother C. B., and my best friend in the whole wide world, Betty Jean Drye, Booper. I'll see them again someday, in Heaven.

I also want to include my sister Betty Vaughn Miles and her children, my sisters Sheila Ann and Shirley Jan Jeffcoat and their children, and all my nieces and nephews: Gerald, Gary Wayne, Brenda, Lynn, Sherrie, and Michelle, and all of their children. Wow, what a family, and I love them all dearly. And then there's me: the buck stops here. I'm the old maid of the family. Then there are my cousins, but there's not enough room in the book for all of them!

And I would be remiss if I didn't thank my Hurstettes, June Cochran, Nikki Phillips, Shelley Harmon Bell, Marsha Bennett, Tami Pittman, and all the rest. We were quite the team and I miss those days at the track with them.

People occasionally ask me why I never posed nude for *Playboy* or *Penthouse*, or one of those magazines. They all tried to get me, but I turned them all down. I promised my mother two things in my life. One of them was, she once said, "I want you to promise me you'll never do anything to embarrass the family."

I told her, "I'll always make you proud of me and I'd never do anything to embarrass the family. I'm going to make a lot more money keeping my clothes on!" And I did.

The other promise was when she watched me race in the Skip Barber Series at Laguna Seca. I did very well, but it scared the hell out of her and she made me promise to never do it again. So I did.

The last thing on this earth I ever wanted to do was disappoint my wonderful mother. She was my whole life and was always there for me, and with me, every step along this journey I've taken. A professional seamstress, she was my "costume designer" for nearly everything I wore in the early days, and she also did all of my Hurstettes' clothes. She's still with me always, in spirit, and so is C. B., Brenda, and Booper.

My Loves

I've had a few loves in my life, for sure, but I'm not one to kiss and tell and this book is not going to be salacious and discuss my love life. Maybe someday I'll write that book, or maybe not. But I should be forthcoming about some of the men who meant a great deal to me. Without mentioning any details, I can say that the loves of my life included the amazing Jim

Page 209 and above: They had a birthday party for Carroll Shelby at the Petersen Automotive Museum and I dressed up as Marilyn Monroe and sang "Happy Birthday" to him, like Marilyn did to President Kennedy. On the left is Lynn Park of the Shelby club.

My current boss Craig Schantz of Chevrolet Performance and I before the start of the Indianapolis 500. It's an honor working with Chevrolet and Craig. He's extremely professional and a gentleman and puts on a great show. (Tom Siefker Photo)

"I'm not exaggerating. There were between 30 and 50 lined up to get her autograph at my high school reunion!"

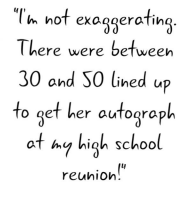

Clark, Tim Richmond (TLR my Superstar), Daniel Ezekiel Ongais, and my ex-husband Billy Tidwell.

I can't say that Tidwell was an actual "love of my life," but he is the only man that I ever married. I met him in 1970 at the drag races in Bakersfield. He was a brown-eyed, handsome Top Fuel driver, standing by that dragster with all that curly hair, smiling at me. He said, "I got something to show you" and pulled a picture of me out of his billfold, and I about fainted. He asked me out on a date and we dated almost all of that year, and got married in 1972.

We were married for 13 years, and that was a long enough sentence! We started a rep business, but as things went wrong I tried to make them right, and considering the business, I stayed way too long. It was very tough, very hard, and I made a decision that I didn't want to have any children in our volatile situation and went back to work really hard and heavy. We got divorced in 1986; I say I "got 86'd in '86."

It was so stressful that I got sick and thought I had cancer, and was in the hospital. But it wasn't cancer; the stress was so much that I became deathly ill and lost 64 pounds. While I was in the hospital, Hurst was bought out by Joe Hrudka at Mr. Gasket and I thought I was out of a job, but I got a phone call from Joe and Carroll Shelby.

Shelby said, "Linder! I got Joe here with me. You want a job?"

I said, "Hell yes, if he buys Hurst."

Shelby said, "Well, he just did."

I received a contract and a salary that allowed me to keep my house and when I woke up in the hospital, Tidwell was standing at the foot of my bed and I said, "You're out of my life. The only cancer was you." And I never looked back. I still see him occasionally and I'm polite to him. I *have* thought about running him over, but I won't.

My current relationship is with Greg Chamberlain, and we've been dating for 18 years now.

Greg Chamberlain on Linda Vaughn

When I was in high school, a few buddies and I went to Lions Drag Strip to watch the drag races, and sometime during the day they announced, "Ladies and gentlemen, we'd like to introduce Linda Vaughn, Miss Hurst Golden Shifter." We didn't know who she was but she came out in a 2-piece gold bathing suit and we were just completely amazed.

The next time I saw her was a few years later, in my 20s, when I went to Irwindale with my dad. She was there and my dad said, "Do you know her? That's some woman right there."

I said, "No. I'd sure like to, though."

The next time I saw her was in 1989 or 1990. I bought a Harley and a friend and I rode our bikes out to Pomona for the drags, and we were walking through the pits and my buddy nudged me and said, "Check it out." It was Linda. She was dressed like Stevie Ray Vaughn, with black tights, a black hat, and black high-heel boots. She looked amazing. I stared at her and she looked back at me and we just held each other's gaze for a while. It was almost like a stare-down contest.

Some years later, another friend called me and said, "You have to come over here and meet this girl." I had a date that night, but my buddy kept on my butt about it, so I went over to his house for a few minutes just to shut him up. The girl turned out to be Linda. We both looked at each other and it was love at first sight. We hit it off right away. She had a date with the singer Johnny Rivers that night but forgot about it and I forgot about my date, and we sat at my friend's house just talking until 5:00 am. Since that night we haven't been apart.

It was something neither one of us expected. We went together for about six months before I even kissed her. We became friends, so it was very different than the typical scene with other girls. There was much more to it than just physical attraction.

We have traveled the world together and experienced a lot of new things, and we're there for each other no matter what the other needs. I've been to Georgia and met her family. Her brother and a few of his country friends weren't sure what to make of me, but when they tested my shooting ability, I think I impressed them and became part of the family.

We went to my 40th high school reunion together, which was a lot of fun. When we walked into the place, everyone turned and looked at Linda. That same group of guys I went to Lions with in high school was all there, and I walked up to one of them and said, "Remember when we were at the drags?"

And he stared at Linda and said, "No s**t, that's her!"

I'm not exaggerating. There were between 30 and 50 lined up to get her autograph; at *my* high school reunion!

I have a boyfriend and we've been dating each other for 18 years now. His name is and we are pretty good companions and see eye-to-eye on a lot of matters, but on some matters we don't so he lives in his house and I live in mine. I take care of him when he is sick and he took care of me with my recent heart issues. I can't live with him and I can't live without him.

"I obviously believe in angels because I hand out my Pocket Angels to any racers, to help keep them safe."

The only man that I ever lived with for 17 years, my cat Snow bringing me a flower. He was 16 years old and pretty sick in this photo, and died a year later.

About My Memory

People often comment about my memory; I have an ability to remember not just people's names but also details about them. I've been asked how I do it, and I honestly don't know. I just want to, I guess. I would try to relate them to what car they drove or what product they represented, what shifter they used, what brakes they used. I'd try to keep it all covered in my mind. I didn't have a computer, my mind was my computer.

I would go with the gang but I've never been a drinker, and that helped me remember everything. While everybody else was getting drunk and forgetting stuff, I'd remember everything. Jack Duffy was so funny; we'd be walking through the pits the next day and he'd say, "Okay, who's that approaching us?" and I'd say, "That's Bill Broderick from Union 76, that's Dick Dolan with the Pure Oil Company, there's Bob Anderson over there with Chrysler, and here comes Ronnie."

I remember all their names because I associated them with the cars or with their products. Unfortunately, as I'm getting older I can't remember things quite as well as I used to. I'm still pretty good at it, but there are times when I see someone and I know I should know them but can't put a name to the face, and that's frustrating.

More About Me

When it comes to music, I love all kinds of country, classical, blues, and good black gospel music. I used to slip off and go to the black churches every Sunday when I was a little girl. My personal favorite musicians are Willie Nelson, Neil Diamond, Huey Lewis, Bob Seger, Keb Mo, and Ray Charles. They are all great personal friends of mine, and I even got Willie to play SEMA one year. And rock and roll? AC/DC, Bonjovi, Rolling Stones, Guns and Roses! I love all kinds of music really, even opera and some jazz.

This is my land in Georgia that daddy left me. I love that piece of property and can't wait to go home. My sister's house is just up the hill.

My gorgeous niece Lynn Vaughn and my handsome brother C. B. I lost my brother at 73 to a heart condition similar to mine and I dearly miss him. When he came to the Indianapolis 500 he signed autographs for people thinking he was the actor Richard Egan. Lynn is down in Florida today selling real estate.

One of the things I don't care for is talking politics and religion because it's nobody else's business, but I have faith. I believe in the Almighty and angels, and I have angels all over my house. I obviously believe in angels because I hand out my Pocket Angels to any racers I can, to help keep them safe. My scruples are in the right place and I'm very faithful so I'll leave it at that.

As for politics, again I don't like to go into details but I'm of the firm opinion that we need to clean up America. I think America should go back to believing in their faith and clean up America, and do it with cars too. I think our country was built on "In God We Trust" and we need to go back to that. It saddens me now to see what's happening in America today; it saddens me to see what's happening with our youth. It saddens me to go on the freeway and see that I'm driving the only American car out of 10. It all just saddens me.

If I were president, the first thing I'd do is put Detroit back to work and build pride in the country again. I'd control the unions with hard-working people with pride like Ford has done, clean up America, put the armed forces on our borders, and go into the school system and educate kids for the future of America. And of course, I'd rekindle our love affair with the automobile. And if you're going to live in America, speak English. That's my belief. What would make me happy is to see Americans fall in love with America again. Manufacturing is what America was built on and we need to bring it back.

When it comes to food, I like Southern food because that's where I'm from. Not in restaurants but real Southern food made in the South; good old-fashioned home-cooked meals. My mother was the best cook, and she taught me. She could bake anything and barbecue anything in her old-fashioned oven. I couldn't believe what came out of that oven.

This is Gerald and Juli Vaughn. Gerald is my brother C. B.'s boy and has carried on the Vaughn family name. Gerald loves to go to the races and to Barrett Jackson with me. Gerald took up calling me Linder after he heard Carroll Shelby call me that. He even had a Hurst Olds!

These were Greg's dogs when I first started dating him. The blonde one is Casey, the momma, and the black one is Olive, just the cutest ever. Greg had them for a long time before we got together but they passed away and now we have a new dog together, Curly Joe Cocker, the most beautiful brown Cocker Spaniel I've ever seen.

This is my dog, Curley Joe. He's my baby.

"Grumpy was a connoisseur of great food and the last meal I made for him and my boyfriend Greg was beef stroganoff."

She taught me well. I love to make homemade biscuits, cornbread, fried potatoes, turnip greens. And I *love* vegetables. I most enjoy cooking when I have the support of the people I'm cooking for. Grumpy was a connoisseur of great food and the last meal I made for him and my boyfriend Greg was beef stroganoff. I took a New York strip steak and grilled it, then sliced it diagonally and put it in my iron skillet with sour cream and my fabulous mushroom gravy, and served it with some nice potatoes. Grumpy absolutely loved the meal and brought a $200 bottle of wine to go with my beef stroganoff!

I love French, Italian, Armenian, and Jewish food too. Basically I just love good food. But what I don't like is liver. No way. I can't stand it and I'm not eating it. I'm definitely carnivorous. I love good char-grilled beef, chicken, fish, and grilled salmon, and especially an old-fashioned meatloaf. I'm an old-fashioned meat and potatoes girl, can't you tell?

And did you know that grits stands for "Girls Raised In the South"? See what grows when you eat grits? And I've eaten a lot of grits as you can see!

Final Thoughts

I have been asked many times if I will ever retire and my standard answer is that I might retire when I die. But then I'm sure I'll raise up out of the casket and say, "Is anybody going to Daytona or Pomona?" In reality, I'd like to slow down and just make some special appearances like the auctions; the General Motors, Chrysler, and Ford appearances; and maybe a couple of IndyCar and NASCAR races.

I just want to stay off airplanes because I can't seem to get well. I haven't been in the best of health for the last dozen years or so and it's been bothering me a lot. Plus without my pension I have to keep working. And I do love it.

But I'm living my life the way I want to live it. There's nobody else so I'm going to do it my way, and my greatest treasures are my memories. They can't take your memories away from you.

This is such a magnificent photo. Little George from Sports Illustrated *shot this during a photo shoot I was doing in the early 1980s. And no, it wasn't for the swimsuit issue. I didn't have a swimsuit or anything on under that! It's one of the most beautiful photos, but I was freezing my butt off!*

I like to go the Moonshine Festival in Dawsonville, Georgia, whenever I can, which is where this photo was taken. On the left is Wanda Lund (Tiny Lund's wife), with Doris Roberts (Fireball's wife) on the far right, and me in one of my Bill Simpson outfits.

Courtney Hansen is a good friend of mine and we work together a lot. She works as a television spokesperson, probably best known for hosting the show Overhaulin' with Chip Foose, but she's done things for NASCAR among others. I love Courtney and her family; Daddy "Jerry," the greatest SCCA driver.

Here I am with David Pearson and his black 1940 Ford hot rod at the Moonshine Festival. David is one of the first racers that I was in Victory Circle with. He's a great friend and I'm proud to know the Pearson family. He's my sister Betty's favorite driver.

This is with Jack Smith at the Moonshine Festival. Jack drove for Pontiac in 1962 when I was Miss Pontiac.

My mother and I with Wally and Barbara Parks at the NHRA Hot Rod Reunion in Bakersfield, California, posing in front of my hot rod Lincoln. My mother was great friends with Barbara and Wally and we were especially proud to be at Wally's Hot Rod Reunion, which is what I called it. I go every year.

This was taken at my sister Betty's 80th birthday party at Gerald Vaughn's home. That's Sheila on the left and Shirley behind us.

In my driveway at home with my hot rod Lincoln. I built the Lincoln with my boys: Guy Caldwell and Edsel Ford got me the engine, a 32-valve V-8 from a Lincoln Mark VIII mounted in the back like a Ferrari, Gene Winfield painted it, and Carroll Shelby finished it up for me. We made the SEMA Car of the Year the same year as the Plymouth Prowler.

We built a hot rod that was affordable for people to power with either a Ford, Chevy, Cadillac, Oldsmobile, or any engine. I wanted to have something affordable for American engines. I tell women when it's at a show, "There sits my facelift, my tummy tuck, my swimming pool, and my fence around my house!" It took nine months to build so it was like giving birth, but I'm glad I built it. My boyfriend Greg Chamberlain took the photo.

"But I'm living my life the way I want to live it. There's nobody else so I'm going to do it my way, and my greatest treasures are my memories. They can't take your memories away from you. Only God can."

Posing in a new Simpson outfit that I wore in the pits at the Indianapolis 500. You really need a firesuit in the pits so I came up with the design and Bill Simpson made it for me.

This is on Greg's 1986 Harley-Davidson Softail. I hadn't ridden in 14 years until we took these pictures. I was hurt once on a bike, broke my wrist, so I was very careful.

INDEX

A

Adams, Jackie Hart, 83
Agajanian Special, 178
Agajanian, J. C., 44, 142, 178
AHRA, 91, 93, 105, 113, 175, 207
Aikman, Troy, 135
Airheart, Bob, 44, 46, 47, 52, 54, 57, 64, 90, 143, 192, 197, 205
Alderman, Elton, 193
Alexander, Tyler, 155
Allison, Arthur C., 140
Allison, Bobby, 129
Allison, Davey, 21, 124
Allison, Donnie, 134
Allison, James A., 140
Allison, Judy, 39
Alloway, Bobby, 202
Amato, Joe, 198
Anderson, Loni, 186, 212
Andretti, Mario, 38, 80, 99, 145, 156, 161, 164, 166, 171, 173, 176, 196
ARCA, 35, 120
Armstrong, Neil, 67
Arons, Dick, 200
Arute, Jack, 156
Atlanta Motor Speedway, 118, 126
Atlanta Raceway, 25, 27–31, 34, 117, 118
Aumack, Capt., 66

B

Baja Boot, 152
Baker, Buddy, 41
Barris, George, 185, 192, 194, 201, 203
Baryshnikov, Mikhail, 188
Batmobile, 201
Beadle, Raymond, 21, 91, 96, 98
Bell, Shelley Harmon, 71, 72, 75, 79, 129, 147, 208
Bellino, Gino, 69
Benetton Tyrrel team, 156
Bennett, Gary, 202
Bennett, Marsha, 60, 71, 72, 74, 78, 208
Bernstein, Kenny, 98, 107, 201
Bettenhausen, Gary, 146
Big Bauty, 61
Bigelow, Tom, 38
Bignotti, George, 60, 198

Biow, Milton, 40
Bishop, Dave, 200
Black, Jack and Glenda, 13, 17, 22–24, 27, 31, 48, 51, 61, 73, 89, 117, 151, 176, 211, 212, 214, 216
Blackstock, Shelby, 188
Blue Max, 91, 96
Bonnet, Neil, 195
Booth, Wally, 53, 115, 130, 200, 203
Brabham, Geoff, 173, 198
Brakefield, Bill and Marion, 195
Brizio, Roy, 202
Brock, Peter, 179
Brock, Ray, 51, 84, 178
Burman, Bob, 140
Byron, Red, 123

C

Cagan, Leo, 47
Caldwell, Guy, 217
Camp, Larry, 120, 195
Candies, Paul, 98
Capps, Ronnie, 170, 196
Carlton, Gigi, 191
Carpenter, Al, 47, 50, 68, 189
CART, 72, 76, 142, 159, 178
Case, Robby, 20, 47, 52
Caviezel, Jim, 187
Caylor, James, 131
Cayuga International Speedway, 129
Chamberlain, Greg, 38, 198, 210, 211, 214, 217, 218
Chapman, Colin, 154, 196
Charles, Ray, 23, 44, 108, 212
Charlotte, 23, 25, 34, 35, 40, 51, 123, 135
Chernoff, Dr. Greg, 161, 208
Childress, Richard, 130
Chrysler, Richard, 51, 122
Clark, Jim, 65, 154, 155, 171, 173, 176, 177, 210
Cochran, June, 51, 63, 71–73, 80, 82, 111, 141, 208
Coker, Corky, 194
Collins, Sid, 141
Colter, Jessie, 100
Conrad, Pete, 67
Conrad, Robert, 181, 182, 183
Cooper, Gordon, 67
Couch, Buster, 24, 88, 96, 101, 127
Coughlin, GaGa, 102

Coughlin, Mike, 114
Coughlin, Jeg Jr., 102
Coughlin, Jeg Sr., 100, 102
Crawford, Rick, 131

D

Darlington, 31, 33, 39, 41
Davis, Steve, 201, 202
Delrose, Tim, 134
Denver, John, 148, 181
Detroit Auto Show, 13, 42
Diamond, Neil, 65, 212
Dietz, Jim, 89
Dillon, Austin, 130
Dolan, Dick and Betty, 32, 38, 41, 212
Donahue, Mark, 154
Dragway 42, 108
Drake, Dale, 141
Draper, Mr. and Mrs., 47
Drevo, Bill, Jr., 200
Drye, Betty Jean, 32, 36, 43, 208
Drye, Meeka, 38
Duffy, Jack, 37, 44, 46–48, 52, 53, 55, 57, 65, 71, 74, 78, 81, 87, 90, 135, 137, 140, 163, 169, 205, 212
Dunbar, Cheryl, 13
Dunn, Jim, 99

E

Earnhardt, Dale, 12, 117, 123, 127, 129, 136
Eastwood, Clint, 33
Economaki, Chris, 28, 143
Edlebrock, Vic, 192, 197
Eidy, Sam, 194
Elliott, Bill, 197, 199
Els, Chesney, 201
Endervite, Jimmy, 143, 154, 176

F

Fish, Sal, 51, 120, 123, 193, 214
Fishel, Herb, 192
Fisher, Carl G., 140
Follmer, George, 178, 198
Folsom, Danny, 152
Foose, Chip, 216
Force, Courtney, 104
Force, John, 16, 196
Fortune, Blackie, 134, 155
Foster, Pat, 86, 91
Fox, Ray, 17

Foyt, A. J., 35, 49, 54, 72, 99, 127, 134, 141, 144, 154, 156, 162, 173, 179, 201

France, Bill, 50, 66, 82, 117, 120, 124, 196

Franchitti, Dario, 104, 161, 165, 171

Freight Train, 93

G

Gage, Dennis, 63

Ganassi, Chip, 62, 99, 149, 189, 196, 203

Gapp, Wayne, 130

Garlits, Don, 21, 22, 24, 89, 91, 92, 95, 96, 187, 205

Garlits, Pat, 92

Garner, James, 47, 61, 82, 110, 151, 152, 154, 159, 160, 163, 175, 177

George, Mary Hulman, 164, 168

George, Nancy, 125, 127, 153, 158, 161, 164, 165, 166, 170, 171, 188, 195, 196

George, Tony, 137, 187

Giampetroni, Angelo, 182, 185, 192, 202

Giampetroni, Kathleen, 182, 183, 193

Gibbons, Billy, 193

Glick, Shav, 198

Goldsmith, Paul, 49, 179

Gordon, Robby, 67, 125, 128, 130, 165, 178

Grant, Crash, 31, 74

Green, Ben and Sally, 91, 164, 171

Greene, Lorne, 39, 187

Gregory, Amos, 24, 35

Gregory, Julian, 24

Grotheer, Don, 60

Grumpy's Toy, 95

Gurney, Dan, 47, 118, 143, 170, 196

Gurney, Effie, 143

Gwynn, Darrell, 99, 103, 196, 201

Gwynn, Jerry, 103

H

Haines, Jim, 141

Hairy Olds, 51–53, 89, 90

Hamilton, Pete, 118

Hansen, Courtney, 62–63, 127, 166, 170, 216

Harrell, Dickey, 60, 91

Harroun, Ray, 152

Harsh, Phil, 135

Hart, C. J., 83, 85

Hearns, Thomas, 49

Helton, Mike, 136, 149, 203

Hemi Under Glass, 65, 66, 68, 89, 90, 137

Hill, Graham, 104, 143, 154, 176

Hill, Roy, 97, 98

Hillbilly, 97

Hobbs, Leonard C. and Jennifer, 54

Hobbes, Sir David, 172

Hogan, John, 102, 111

Holland, Tammy, 193

Holman, John, 29, 34

Holman, Ralph, 34

Hope, Bob, 66, 67, 136, 149, 152, 203, 205

Hrudka, Joe, 52, 54, 86, 194, 197, 210

Hubbard, Red, 51, 66

Hudgins, Huggie, 24

Hulman, Tony, 141, 143, 152, 153, 159, 164, 168

Hulman, Tony Jr., 152

Hulme, Denny, 155, 179

Hurst, George, 37, 50, 51, 54, 57, 60, 61, 68, 81, 83, 84, 86, 87, 89, 90, 93, 109, 118, 130, 141, 154, 163, 183, 185, 194, 202, 205

Hurst, Lila, 50, 68

Hurst, Pam, 81, 83

Hurtubise, Jim, 150

I

IHRA, 93, 175, 205

Indianapolis Motor Speedway, 37, 38, 61, 82, 110, 123, 127, 137, 139–141, 143, 146, 150, 152–154, 157, 159–163, 168, 173, 150, 153, 155–157, 161, 168, 169, 173

International Motorsports Hall of Fame, 15, 49, 192, 202

IROC, 117, 137, 144, 168, 176, 177

J

Jackson, Craig, 197, 201, 202

Jackson, Sandy, 195

Jeffcoat, Kenneth Lee, 18, 19, 21

Jeffcoat, Sheila Ann, 21, 81, 208

Jeffcoat, Shirley Jan, 18, 19, 21, 208

Jenkins, Bill, 21, 79, 95, 96, 99, 155

Johns, Bobby, 121

Johns, Lori, 199

Johnson, Junior, 21, 29, 99, 179

Jones, Henry, 135

Jones, Jack, 107

Jones, Parnelli, 44, 84, 178, 203

Judge, Judi, 31, 34, 83, 199

K

Kagan, Leo, 192

Karamesines, Chris, 30

Kelly, Susie and Jim, 53, 76, 77, 113

Kerr, Jimmy, 192

Keys, Bobby, 60, 189

King, Jimmy, 22, 49, 125, 126, 152, 200

Knight, Michael, 196

Krauss, Billy, 179

Krieger, Mike, 206

L

Langley, Elmo, 40, 119

Lanier, Randy, 162

Lassiter, General Dick, 65

Lawford, Jim, 200

LeMay, General Curtis, 65

Lewis, Huey, 212

Lincoln Speedway, 45, 55, 98, 119, 185, 217

Lions Drag Strip, 107, 187, 211

Lippencott, Floyd Jr., 203

Lipper, Ray, 192

Lombardo, John, 21, 115

Lorenzen, Fred, 21, 28, 29, 31, 39, 118, 121

Louise, Edwina, 12, 20, 21, 43, 49, 122

Lund, Tiny, 21, 120, 131

Lund, Wanda, 126, 216

M

MacGillivray, Peter, 21, 120, 126, 131, 216

Mancheski, Fred, 202

Maple Grove Raceway, 103

Marciano, Rocky, 49

Marcum, John, 35, 120

Marlin, Sterling, 135, 136

Martin, Buddy, 22, 96, 102, 115

Martinsville Speedway, 37

Maseles, Howard, 44

Mathews, Banjo, 134

Mazmanian, John, 74

McCardle, Bob, 200

McClurg, Bob, 31, 57, 73, 80, 81, 82, 88, 112, 113

McClusky, Roger, 142

McCullough, Ed, 115

McDonald, Davey, 153, 154

McEntire, Reba, 188

McFarland, Charles, 23

Mecom, John, 143, 154, 163

Meyer, Billy, 98, 135, 203

Milk Wagon, 23

Miller, Ken, 30, 161

Miskotten, Carl, 133

Mitchell, Jackie, 23

Mitchell, Tom, 131

Mo, Keb, 212

Moffett, Jimmy, 122

Moon, Dean, 88, 142

Moore, Bud, 129

Moore, Marla, 193

Moscone, Tommy, 119

Mother, 12, 13, 15–22, 24, 27, 31–33, 35, 38, 39, 48, 49, 51, 52, 55, 57, 58, 61, 63–65, 71, 75, 81, 82, 86, 92, 96, 97, 99, 100, 102, 106, 107, 109, 110, 112, 120, 123–127, 130, 136, 141, 143, 147, 148, 150, 158, 160, 163, 169, 170, 172, 182, 186, 189, 194, 198, 201, 203, 207, 208, 213, 217

Mr. Gibb, 91

Muldowney, Shirley, 89, 101, 108, 109, 111

Mullinax, Benjamin Franklin, 22

Muravez, Bob, 203

Museum of Speed, 45

Myle, Tom, 200

N

Nabors, Jim, 143, 157, 159, 160, 186

Naman, Don, 195

Nance, Robert, 23

NASCAR, 33, 35, 39, 41, 50, 51, 62, 63, 79, 90, 94, 96, 97, 110, 117, 120–124, 128, 129, 133, 136, 137, 140, 143, 149, 152, 156, 158, 175, 176, 178, 195, 201–203, 205, 214, 216

Neely, Bill, 151, 159, 173, 186

Nelson, Willie, 28, 202, 212
Newberry, Jimmy, 18, 23, 24, 25
Newberry, Josephine, 40
Newberry, Linda, 18, 23–25, 40
Newby, Arthur C., 140
New York Auto Show, 51, 54, 83
Nicholson, Don, 91, 160

O

Old Blue, 86
Olson, Ozzy, 118
Ongais, Daniel Ezekiel, 86, 148, 176, 177, 198, 210
Orange County International Raceway, 93, 95
Ostrove, Billy, 68
Ottum, Bob, 186

P

Padgett, Mike, 125
Panch, Marvin, 120
Park, Lynn, 89, 210
Parker, Dottie, 34, 37, 140, 187
Parks, Barbara, 101, 217
Parks, Wally, 50, 85, 107, 115, 197, 217
Parsons, Benny, 129
Paschal, Jim, 29
Patrick, Danica, 158, 160, 164
Pearson, David, 20, 21, 118, 137, 216
Penske, Roger, 98, 144, 148, 154, 181
Petersen, Robert E., 85, 191, 203, 210
Petty, Kyle, 21, 200
Petty, Linda, 21, 39, 126
Petty, Maurice, 97
Petty, Richard, 16, 20, 21, 39, 49, 53, 97, 99, 119, 122, 126, 137, 153, 156,
Phillips, Nikki, 71, 72, 77, 79, 81, 91, 208
Pickle, Grady, 22
Pink, Ed, 95, 101
Pittman, Tami, 80, 99, 115, 208
Platt, Hubert, 44, 94, 102
Plunkett, Steve, 63
Polamalu, Troy, 188
Pocono Raceway, 53, 54, 72, 140, 145, 158
Proffitt, Hayden, 68

Prudhomme, Don, 95, 96, 110, 194
Purcell, Usona and Hilda, 134

R

Rahal, Bobby, 160, 164, 198
Rahal, Graham, 104,
Ramchargers, 108
Rawlings, Rich, 192
Reinhardt, Alan, 115
Revson, Peter, 152, 155
Reynolds, Burt, 124, 160, 186
Richey, Earl, 44, 47
Richmond, Timothy Larry, 137, 150, 186, 208, 210
Rickenbacker, Eddie, 152
Rife, Hilly, 119, 122
Riggle, Bob, 65, 66, 68, 89, 90
Riley, Joe, 200, 201
Ripes, Marv, 200
Riverside International Raceway, 51, 52, 72, 73, 84, 111, 117, 123, 143, 177, 181, 198
Roberts, Doris, 20, 21, 31, 34, 39, 121, 126, 205, 216
Roper, Jim, 123
Roush, Jack, 98, 130
Roventini, Johnny, 40
Ruby, Lloyd, 13, 15, 38, 142
Russo, Bob, 198
Ruth, Carl, 196, 200
Rutherford, Johnny, 150

S

Sabates, Felix, 130
Sachs, Eddie, 153, 154
Sanders, Clare, 108
Schantz, Craig, 210
Schiefer, Paul, 44, 46, 52, 64, 98, 107, 205
Schrader, Ken, 126, 134, 136
Schropshier, Forrest, 23
Schubeck, Joe, 51, 53, 89, 179, 191, 203
Schultz, Kenny, 200
Schumacher, Don, Larry, and Tony, 102
Schwartz, Gerry, 91
Seger, Bob, 212
SEMA, 47, 53, 57, 60, 62, 67, 89, 90, 95, 179, 183, 185, 191-194, 197, 202, 203, 212, 217
Setzer, Barry, 102
Shadinger, Pete, 200
Shelby, Carroll, 38, 69, 179,

188, 193-195, 197, 198, 201, 203, 210, 213, 217
Shrewsberry, Bill, 90
Simpson, Bill, 37, 82, 136, 137, 154, 162, 198, 216, 218
Sinbad, 202
Sirokan, Mike, 90, 92
Siroonian, Richard, 74
Skinner, Mike, 201
Slack, Bob, 129
Smith, Bill, 49, 158, 192, 197, 216
Smith, Bruton, 158
Smith, Don, 192
Snider, George, 171
Snyder, Janice, 29
Sox, Ronnie, 21, 96, 102, 115
Sox & Martin, 96, 115
Spar, Bobby, 192
Stalker, Trudi, 123, 126, 127, 130, 131, 196, 201
Stewart, Sir Jackie, 62, 66, 127, 128, 143, 177, 196, 200
St. James, Lyn, 43, 158, 164, 196
Stone, Sharon, 197, 201
Sullivan, Tim, 135, 156

T

Talladega, 41, 126, 172, 186, 192, 195
Tharp, Richard, 96
Thompson, Mickey, 21, 86, 91, 107, 176, 177, 179
Tice, Jim, 91
Tilton, Ron, 44, 47
Toundas, Peter, 202
Trickle, Dick, 129
Truesdell, Ray, 49
Tuller, Goober, 93
Tullius, Bob, 77, 83
Tyson, Mike, 49

U

Unser, Al, 60, 142, 148, 158, 166, 168, 172, 173, 181, 188, 189,
Unser, Bobby, 47, 196, 198
Unser, Shelley, 188
USAC, 134, 142, 178

V

Vanke, Arlen, 104
Van Winkle, Rob, 188

Vaughn, Betty Louise, 11, 12, 14, 15, 19, 20, 22, 24, 31, 47, 50, 51, 54, 62, 63, 69, 76, 77, 80, 81, 89, 97, 99, 104, 112, 113, 125, 128, 131, 134, 143, 145, 152, 155, 156, 158, 164, 171, 178, 179, 184, 197-199, 206, 208, 211, 213, 217
Vaughn, C. B. Jr,
Vaughn, Gerald, 197, 208, 213, 217
Vaughn, Mae, 12, 15, 16, 112, 160
Vaughn, Sam A., 14, 19
Vaughn, Seabrun, 12
Vaughn, Sean, 125
Vukovich, Bill, 35

W

Walker, Clint, 33, 41
Wall, Marcia, 20, 28, 51, 78, 148, 157, 158, 169
Wallace, Rusty, 130, 203
Wangers, Jim, 50
Watson, Jack, 51, 61, 106
Wawak, Bobby, 135
Weaver, Nelson, 28
Wells, Dick, 67, 191, 197
Wheat, Lt. Cmdr., 66
Wheeler, Frank H., 140
Whitener, Billie, 129
Whitlock, Joe, 123
Wiebe, John, 105
Winfield, Gene, 217
Wolfe, Tom, 29

X

Xydias, Alex, 197

Y

Yarborough, Cale, 39, 119, 122
Yardley race team, 155
Yates, Brock, 187, 193
Yates, Robert, 124
Yowell, Bobby, 17
Yowell, Neil, 112
Yunick, Smokey, 20

Z

Zinkhan, Bill, 200
Zoeller, Fuzzy, 189

Additional books that may interest you...

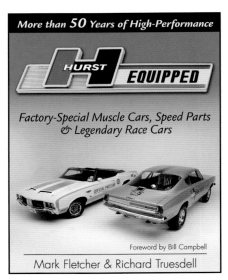
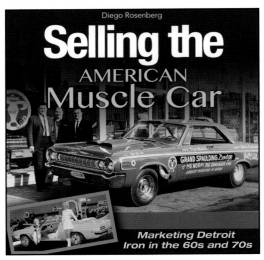

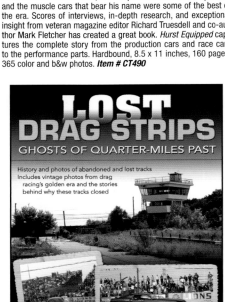